Living Grace

*A Daily Companion for
Meditation and Contemplation*

Craig Bullock

(Isha Das)

Copyright © 2016 Craig Bullock

All rights reserved.

ISBN: 1539769771
ISBN-13: 978-1539769774

DEDICATION

For Nicholas and Michael – my beloved sons and very good friends.

4/3 + 4/4 SAME MEDITATION

ACKNOWLEDGEMENTS

My litany of saints includes many generous people whose support accompanied me at every stage in the preparation of this book.

I'm grateful to my wife, Vickijo, for her constant encouragement, enthusiasm, and love. I'm also grateful to my big Italian family who allow me the necessary space and time to write.

Mary McFee painstakingly edits these reflections on a daily basis. In addition, she took on the enormous task of sifting through years of compiled reflections and choosing those most appropriate for this publication. Without her editorial skills and devotion this book would not exist. Thank you, Mary, for being the blessing that you are to the Assisi Institute and to me.

I'm also very appreciative of the staff at the Assisi Institute. I am indebted to our Swami, Purnima, for the depth of her faithfulness to Paramahansa Yogananda and to the path of Kriya Yoga. Purnima, your consciousness helps to sustain me. Thank you to Adam Reitz for your friendship, honesty, and artistic talent, which is displayed on the cover of this book. You are a tremendous gift to our organization. I also want to lovingly acknowledge Ursula Arnold. Her love, compassion, and gentle strength bring joy to all of us.

Last but not least, I want to thank my spiritual brothers and sisters within The Assisi Institute family. Every day I thank God for the privilege of serving God and guru alongside of you. It is a profound blessing to meditate with you, to pray with you, to laugh with you, to suffer with you, and to be a source of healing for the world with you. Thank you.

Living Grace

CONTENTS

JANUARY
The Divine Mother	1
The Guru	7
Transformation	13
Trust	19
Silence	25
The Guru	30

FEBRUARY
Meditation	32
Perpetually in God	37
Love	41
Living Spiritually	53

MARCH
Into the Wilderness	61
Temptation	65
Fasting	66
Silence	71
The Past	77
Shame	78
The Body	79
The Illusion of Separation	82
Remember	83
Lazarus	84
Moses	86
The Last Supper	88
The Passion of Jesus	89

APRIL
Waiting in Darkness	92
Resurrection	94
God's Loving Providence	98
The Guru	103
The Present Moment	108
Practicing God's Presence	109

Solitude   118

MAY
The Guru   122
Perpetually in God   125
Fearlessness   132
Judge Not   139
Holy Thinking   142
A Mystical Look at Hell   148
Purgatory: Purification   150
Heaven   151

JUNE
Perpetually in God   153
Intuition   158
Karma   160
I am a Soul   166
Karma Yoga   172
Twelve Steps to Freedom   176

JULY
Twelve Steps to Freedom   183
The Garden   185
Holy Simplicity   188
The Present Moment   192
Meditation   196
Suffering   199
I am a Child of God   202
The Guru   209
Perpetually in God   212

AUGUST
Holy Thinking   214
Facing Our Pain   219
Jesus   223
Healing   227
Happiness   232
Courage   235

Living Grace

Surrender

SEPTEMBER
Moods	245
Yogananda	249
Perpetually in God	253
God Speaks	259
Prayer	264
Living Spiritually	269

OCTOBER
Francis of Assisi	275
I Am a Soul	282
Wounds	285
The Present Moment	288
Temptation	291
Jesus	294
Death	299

NOVEMBER
Truth	306
Transition	311
Grace	315
Silence	319
Mysticism	323
Gratitude	327
God Speaks	333

DECEMBER
The Guru	336
Following the Star	343
The Shepherds	350
The Birth of Jesus	357
Transformation	363

FOREWARD

I am honored to introduce this book of daily reflections, thoughts, and prayers written by my dear friend and spiritual brother, Isha Das – Craig Bullock, founder and spiritual director of The Assisi Institute.

I still remember the joy of my first meeting with Isha Das. It was near the swimming pool during a break at the Kriya Yoga Congress in Atlanta, in 2008. I was surprised to see Craig wearing a necklace with a small Cross of the Tau, which is a Franciscan symbol. Instantly, our souls recognized each other as old friends, meeting after a long journey and renewing the joys of shared experiences of past incarnations.

In this life we live on two different continents, but Isha Das and I have taken up our journey together again, which was interrupted for only a brief time span of a few centuries! We are united by the same destiny wherein every soul perceives the deep meaning of its Being: the moment when the dream ceases and the butterfly starts flying. Our souls have met again to share love for God and the same spiritual teachers, Masters of the East and the West.

Just as it is extremely important for our bodies to consume healthy food and liquid every day, so do our minds need daily servings of positive and inspiring thoughts. Inspired thoughts nourish our souls and infuse hope along our inner path to liberation since "we are what we think." Our dear Isha Das has provided that nourishment in this book.

At present, all of mankind is slowly emerging out of the Kali Yuga, the Dark Age, which is why everyone needs a spiritual tool to awaken his consciousness and proceed quickly to Self and God realization. This is the precious gift of the Kriya Yoga teachings given to us by Babaji, the Father of Kriya Yoga.

Before traveling to America in 1920, Paramahansa Yogananda, our beloved Guru, received some very important tasks from Mahavatar Babaji: to spread Kriya Yoga in the West and to demonstrate to the world the unity between the Gospel of Jesus Christ and the original Yoga philosophy of Sri Krishna, as inscribed in the Bhagavad Gita. Babaji also gave Sri Yukteswar, Yogananda's Guru, a task when they met at the Kumbha Mela in 1894: to write a book that shows the unity underlying all religions. Sri Yukteswar wrote The *Holy Science*, in which he compares the Holy Scriptures of the Vedas and the Revelation of St. John. In 1861, Babaji also instructed his disciple Lahiri Mahasaya to reveal to the world the forgotten teachings of the ancient science of Kriya Yoga. Lahiri Mahasaya taught many of his disciples the sacred technique. On many occasions, Paramahansa Yogananda mentioned that Jesus Christ gave to his closest disciples techniques very similar to Kriya Yoga. This is revealed in the Book of Revelation.

Jesus Christ, Lord Krishna, and all the avatars of different ages brought their messages for the redemption of the world. Through the instruments of Kriya Yoga and the unceasing prayer of the Christian mystics, we are given the daily bread that can feed our starving souls. The daily invocation before meditation that Yoganandaji taught, which deeply focuses our attention on God consciousness, is an expression of gratitude to all those that came before: "Heavenly Father, Divine Mother, Friend, Beloved God, Jesus Christ, Bhagavan Krishna, all Gurus of the Kriya tradition, Guru Preceptor, saints of all religions, we bow to you all." All religions are but different paths leading us to the same one goal.

Living Grace

Yogananda also taught us that meditation techniques are not enough – they must be combined with deep devotion. In fact, an intense love for God is very necessary if we want to get results in our meditation and in our prayers. Having grown up in Calcutta, Yoganandaji was aware of the affirmations of the great saint Sri Ramakrishna who said that God would manifest himself to the devotee who has cried for God unceasingly for 24 hours.

Yoganandaji himself explained the kind of intensity that is necessary to receive an answer from God: "Love Him as a miser loves money, as an ardent man loves his sweetheart, as a drowning person loves breath. When you yearn for God with intensity, He will come to you." Kriya Yoga and devotion for God are the perfect combination for a successful spiritual life.

St. Francis was a living example of the teachings of the Gospel of Christ. We well remember how the saint was asked many times at Fonte Colombo to write the rules for his order so that the monks could follow them. St. Francis, inspired by God, wrote the same words as found in the Gospel but still they were found too difficult to be followed by the complaining friars. Yogananda loved St. Francis of Assisi very much even though the saint was not part of the Kriya tradition. In fact, in him, Yoganandaji saw the image of the perfect disciple who without any hesitation left everything to look for God.

How can St. Francis not be loved? Yoganandaji encouraged all his disciples to follow the living example of St. Francis, the perfect Bhakti Yogi, one who realizes God through devotion. When Yogananda journeyed back to India in 1935, he first visited Europe. Driving through Italy, Yogananda and his little group stopped in Assisi to visit the tomb of St. Francis. He remembered that experience with the following words: "In the morning we reached Assisi. There we saw St. Clare's tomb. St. Clare was a great devotee of St. Francis. St. Francis once broke bread with St. Clare, and while they were sitting together, people from the town saw a blazing light – as if the church was afire. When they came running, the light vanished – it was the light of God."

Yoganandaji continues, "St. Francis met Jesus in the woods almost every night. As I was visiting his living tomb and put my head on the shrine step, St. Francis appeared to me. Then I saw a tunnel of eternity into which he disappeared. The entire cellar beneath the church was replete with vibrations." On another occasion, St. Francis inspired Yoganandaji's beautiful poem, "God, God, God."

Our dear Isha Das has, in an original and inspiring way, united the message of Yogananda and the Kriya tradition with the message of Jesus Christ and mystical Christianity, melting them together in the burning heart of the perfect lover of God, Brother Francis. He has shaped all these elements into a perfect daily inspiration that quenches our thirsty souls.

Every time I visit the Assisi Institute, I feel a deep joy, a sense of the peace of all these hearts searching for God and inspired by Craig's radiant soul. Thank you, Isha Das. With the honey of your love for God you are attracting so many precious souls to Him.

OM Shanti, Shanti, Shantihi,

Swami Nirvanananda Saraswati
Italy, October 7th, 2016

PREFACE

The writing of these reflections began as a desire to offer daily support and encouragement to the members of our spiritual family, The Assisi Institute. That desire has become *Living Grace*, which appears online daily. I write each of these reflections in the same way: After my morning meditation, I read and ponder the words of Jesus, Francis of Assisi, or Paramahansa Yogananda. From a place of prayerful silence, I endeavor to write a simple message that radiates God's truth, beauty, and goodness. This practice has been my routine, day after day, for the past five years. The idea for this book came from a number of people at The Assisi Institute who suggested that we take the best of the daily reflections and compile them into a reader with all the comforts of a book – words, paper, and pages. I pray that it will be a blessing for you.

Craig Bullock

Living Grace

INTRODUCTION

In order to glean as much spiritual nourishment as possible from this book of reflections, I suggest that you begin with a meditation practice. Meditation leads to silence, and silence helps us to be receptive to spiritual inspiration. Therefore, I would like to offer you a transcription of a talk I gave at one of our regular Thursday night Kriya Yoga meditation services. It provides an introduction to a simple meditation practice which can be adapted to any religious tradition or belief system. When done consistently, a meditation practice is a powerful tool for our spiritual evolution. We should always remember that what ultimately makes meditation effective is the devotion, sincerity, and love that we bring to it.

* * *

We speak about meditation often at The Assisi Institute; it is the heart and soul of our spirituality and the heart and soul of Kriya Yoga. The path to God is really very simple. What mother would make it difficult and complicated for her children to come home? No mother would do that, and neither does God.

If you can breathe and think, you can meditate. People say, "I can't quiet my mind." That isn't necessary! Trying to quiet the mind is like wrestling with a tiger; you are going to lose every time. Besides, meditation doesn't work at the level of the mind. It works at the level of the soul and the spirit. So don't be overly concerned if your mind is busy; just let the mind do what it will and take a tiny thread of your awareness and place it on your meditation. Over a period of time, without your trying, your meditation will quiet your mind.

When to meditate? A meditation practice works best if

you do it at about the same time every day. If you cannot do that, any time you meditate is good. But if you get into the habit of meditating at the same time daily, after a period of time your body will be meditating even if you are not. Where to meditate? I like to tell people to take a space, even if it is a corner of a room, and dedicate it to meditation and nothing else. Over a period of time, that meditation space will hold more and more spiritual energy. If you have a guru or a saint that you honor, put a little altar up and place pictures there, if at all possible.

The beginning of meditation is simply to sit. Sit with your head and spine gently aligned, which helps the energy flow up and down the spiritual spine. This posture also creates an alertness which makes us more sensitive to God's presence. In Kriya Yoga, we sit with our hands on our laps and the palms facing the ceiling. This gesture is not merely symbolic; it helps the upward flow of awareness and consciousness to the higher spiritual centers.

Secondly, do something devotional, like prayer or chanting. Yogananda made it very clear that meditation without a devoted heart is not very effective. Say a prayer; ask for God's guidance in the meditation. You may also choose to listen to a chant. In the Kriya tradition, what we recommend is the Gayatri, the oldest and most sacred of all Sanskrit chants.

Now, steady your breath. When we breathe with awareness in a meditative way we are already making conscious contact with God. To steady the breath, inhale slowly, pause, and exhale slowly. Without even trying, you'll notice that your mind grows a little bit quieter. Gently focus your attention on your Third Eye, the point in between your eyebrows.

Notice in the tiny pause between inhalation and

Living Grace

exhalation that there is a little bit of silence.

Continue breathing gently and slowly while touching that silence in between breaths. I recommend that you coordinate your breath with a mantra, and I'm going to suggest either one from the Kriya tradition or one from the Christian tradition.

The Kriya mantra is "Hong Saw." It means, "I am one with that; I am one with God."

On your inhalation, mentally say, "Hong;" pause... and mentally say "Saw" on your exhalation.

If you want a more Christian mantra which is perfectly compatible with Kriya, use the Jesus prayer. On your inhalation mentally say, "Jesus;" pause... and on your exhalation mentally say, "Mercy."

When you feel a little bit of silence and stillness, let it all go and rest. Yogananda says that this resting is the most important part of the meditation. Part of your mind might be active, but that is ok, because another part of your mind will remain aware of the stillness and presence. Just pay attention to the stillness. If you find that your mind kicks in too much, then return to your breath and your mantra to take you back into stillness.

It is that simple!

The last piece of the meditation is saying a prayer of gratitude, such as, "Thank you, God, for this meditation, for its grace and strength. Thank you for another day that I can live for you. At the end of almost all of my meditations I gaze into the eyes of Yogananda, Jesus, or Francis.

Then, a footnote: if you want to do just a little reading

from the scriptures, from Yogananda, from the Bhagavad Gita, do it. In the state of silence, your soul has become permeable and supple, so that what you read will just sink into the cells of your body.

Then, if at all possible, ease in to the rest of your day. Try not to go from meditation directly into stressful environments.

Just a few more words about the silence. Yogananda and the Christian mystics all say the same thing: silence is the most important piece of meditation.

Please don't ever say that you have had a bad meditation. You may have pleasant meditations or unpleasant meditations. If you give God that time, whether you feel like it or not, meditation will help you. Don't look for great signs or seeing angels. You will know it is working because your life will become more peaceful. You will be less reactive and more wise and loving. Success, failure, striving, and competition are not part of a meditation practice. We don't meditate for spiritual experiences, but rather simply because we love God.

* * *

The Divine Mother
January 1

"Behold, I am the handmaiden of the Lord; let it be done to me according to your word."
Mary, the Mother of Jesus

Jesus, Francis and Yogananda have something very important in common: they were each born of a woman. This means that God's love and light always enters the world through a mother. Without the Mother, there is no enlightenment, freedom, or salvation. For this reason, in Catholic and Orthodox Christianity, Mary is the embodiment of the feminine face of God. In fact, her title is "Mother of God." God actually needed Mary's fiat – her Yes in order to wholly enter into human history, in and through Jesus. Her consent to God's overture was the precondition for the marriage of heaven and earth. Thus, Mary is the model of the spiritual life; she teaches us how to give birth to God in our own lives. Just as God needed Mary's Yes to fully break into human affairs, God needs our Yes as well. Such a prayer of consent is neither a superficial nod nor a one-time commitment, but a profound and sustained willingness to surrender all of ourselves to God.

God, Yes.

The Divine Mother

January 2

"So Yogananda brought to this country one of the most important spiritual gifts… the idea of worshiping the Divine Mother."
Kriyananda, a direct disciple of Yogananda

While a third grader attending a Catholic school, I had the unfortunate experience of being expelled – the details of which are not important. Needless to say, my walk home that day was a long one. I anticipated the worst. When I arrived home, my mother was waiting for me. She said two things: "That nun never liked you in the first place," and, "Tomorrow you will have a fresh start in a new school." From that moment forward, my mother had my devotion for all of eternity. Yogananda told his disciples that even the best meditation technique is useless without devotion. Without warmth, tenderness, and compassion, the spiritual life cannot flourish. Only the touch of the Mother creates an opening in our hearts wherein the grace of God may flow. Today, consciously place your attention on an image of the Blessed Mother, the Divine Mother, or someone or something that communicates beauty, care, and love. Allow these gifts to penetrate your heart, thus releasing the grace of God into all areas of your life.

Divine Mother, touch my heart today.

The Divine Mother

January 3

"Your sorrow, your pain, your agony is indeed my sorrow. You and I are two persons and yet you and I are one."
Anandamayi Ma

Once I was given the gift of an icon of the Blessed Mother. I thought it was a nice gift, but not very practical. Then I started meditating on its image. To my surprise, I experienced a deeper, more intimate level of God's presence. I actually sensed that the Divine Mother shares in all our experiences, especially the most painful. In the form of the Divine Mother, God becomes very real, personal, and intimate. Everything we experience, She too experiences. Her unconditional love is fierce, protective, and tender. The Divine Mother is one with us – most especially in our pain, suffering, and grief. Ever approachable, She always responds to our heartfelt pleas and prayers. The compassionate tenderness of the Divine Mother opens us to our own hearts – where the fullness of God's presence is discovered – and frees us from our fearful and confused thinking.

**Divine Mother, give me the grace
to believe that we are one.**

Craig Bullock

The Divine Mother

January 4

"There was a marriage at Cana, and the mother of Jesus was there. When the wine was gone, the mother of Jesus said to him, 'They have no more wine.'"
The Gospel of John

During the marriage feast at Cana, the host found himself in a most embarrassing situation: he ran out of wine. Some might say that this was his karma, that in some way he brought it upon himself. Interestingly, he went to Mary instead of Jesus for help. Why? In this story, Mary clearly represents the loving mercy of God: the Divine Mother. Her blessed role is to unleash heaven's grace into our lives. Without the Mother's grace, there is only karma, which is mechanical in nature. The grace of the Mother is capable of transforming karmic consequences into the freedom and creativity of God's wisdom and power.

Divine Mother, may I always remember your ever-present help.

The Divine Mother

January 5

"Mary said to Jesus, 'They have no more wine.' He answered, 'Woman, what has this to do with me? My hour has not yet come.'"
The Gospel of John

We all have a notion of how our lives should unfold, what should or should not happen according to our preferred timing. However, Mother always knows best. In the gospel story, Jesus was not ready to begin his public ministry. Like us, he had his own notion of when and how his work was going to unfold. Clearly, Mary had another plan in mind. Mary is not a meddling mother, but an instrument through which God speaks – even to override Jesus' plans. What does this mean for us? We are not really in charge of our own lives. The Holy Spirit, God's spirit, runs the show. Divine Mother is the face of the Holy Spirit. Of course we need to plan, but we must ultimately realize that God knows what is best, what will serve our highest evolution, and what is true, beautiful, and good.

Divine Mother, bless me with faith in your plan and your timing.

Craig Bullock

The Divine Mother

January 6

"Mary said to the servants, 'Do whatever Jesus tells you.' The water then became wine."
The Gospel of John

What is it that links us to God's loving and mysterious purposes? How do we avail ourselves of God's influence and power? Inspired, childlike obedience is the key. In the end, Jesus obeys Mary, and the servants obey Jesus. The fruit of his obedience is that the water became the finest of wines. Similarly, God divinizes ordinary human consciousness to overflow with the very consciousness of God. Our English word "obey" comes from the Latin word "obedite," which means "to listen." If we want to experience the wine of God's presence in our lives, we must listen to the Divine Mother's promptings and follow Her guidance. Such holy listening can only occur when we make time for prayer, meditation, and silence. Always be ready to stop, breathe, and listen.

Divine Mother, you are always here, waiting to inspire me.

The Guru

January 7

"You are no longer my servants, but my friends."
Jesus

As a practicing psychotherapist, I am always amazed that people never give up on romance. Even after many divorces, people always seem ready to give marriage another try. Love is what makes us human, what motivates and inspires us. The spiritual life is the greatest of all love affairs. God knows that we humans cannot have a love affair with an impersonal or vague cosmic force, so God wisely comes to us personally in the form of a saint, an avatar, a teacher: a guru. A true guru wants nothing from us; he or she seeks only our highest spiritual evolution. Gurus teach, heal, protect, and intercede. They wait to greet us when we leave this body. The guru makes God real and personal. If we can't love God in a human form, we will never love God as pure, Divine Consciousness. The guru is our heavenly twin who mirrors to us our own divine possibilities.

Oh my guru, come to me.

The Guru

January 8

"God is both impersonal and personal."
Yogananda

Loving the guru is not a sentimental gush of feelings. Rather, loving the guru means that we attune our minds to the guru's wisdom by studying his or her life and teachings. We also attune our will to the gurus' will by bringing ourselves into silence and listening for their direction. Finally, we attune our hearts to their hearts by loving them like a lover does: truly, affectionately, passionately, and constantly. Jesus, Yogananda, Mary the mother of Jesus, Saint Francis, and Anandamayi Ma, among others, act as God's ambassadors. When we follow them as faithful disciples, we love God.

**My Guru, I bow to you
with all the love in my heart.**

The Guru

January 9

"The spiritual soul contact between guru and disciple is one of eternal, unconditional divine love and friendship."
Yogananda

In giving ourselves over to the care of the gurus, we allow them to become our spiritual mothers and fathers. Should we lose our way, they search for us. If we falter, they shower us with divine mercy. If we need guidance, they respond with the very wisdom of God. When it is our time to leave this world, they greet us with open arms. The guru literally carries us so as to bring us home to God, no matter how long the journey may take. The words of Saint Francis to a troubled monk capture perfectly the sweetness and purity of the guru-disciple relationship: "Don't let your thoughts depress you, for you are very dear to me. Know that you are especially dear to me and worthy of my affection and intimacy. Come to me confidently whenever you wish, and don't be afraid to talk to me with utmost familiarity."

**My guru, help me to believe
that I am especially dear to you.**

Craig Bullock

The Guru

January 10

"For we do not have a high priest who is unable to sympathize with us in our weaknesses, but one who in every respect was tempted as we are yet never sinned. Let us then with confidence draw near to the throne of grace, that we may receive mercy and find grace in time of need."
The Book of Hebrews

When we think of gurus and Jesus in particular, we tend to forget that they were human too. They had to travel the same road we travel, face the same challenges we face, and experience exactly what we experience. Though Jesus was completely one with God's consciousness, he was fully human. He was and is one of us, our elder brother. He understands every one of us and why we do the foolish things we do. Therefore, he is forever merciful and compassionate! His merciful compassion, though, is anything but human. Jesus draws from heaven all of the light, grace, strength, wisdom, and love that we need to grow into our own divine potential. Whether we are Christian or not, Jesus' arms are waiting to help, embrace, and love us into Divine Life.

**Jesus, you understand
everything about me.**

The Guru

January 11

"To reestablish God in the temple of souls...is why I was sent to the West."
Yogananda

Young and alone, Yogananda came to the United States in 1920. English was not his first language, he was not Christian, and he had no tangible resources. Yet, he soon attracted thousands of souls who were irresistibly drawn to the sweetness, humility, power, and truth of the small swami from far-away India. Yogananda and his teachings are for all people. Buddhists refer to him as a bodhisattva; Hindus, as an incarnation of God's love; and Christians, as a mystic of the highest order. In Yogananda's blessing, people experience God's guidance, protection, and light. Yet, he never ultimately directs people towards himself, but towards God. He ushers those attuned to him into the very consciousness of Christ and into the Great Silence of God's unspeakable, ineffable presence.

**Guruji, bring God into
the temple of my soul.**

The Guru

January 12

"Blessed are the poor, for the kingdom of God is theirs."
Jesus

One of the most beloved figures in the history of humankind is Francis of Assisi. We know him as a gentle lover of animals, a friend to the poor, an environmentalist, and a man of great joy. These depictions, however, gloss over his radical spirituality. Francis rejected his father's wealth, wore rags, lived in extreme poverty, cleaned the wounds of lepers, fasted, lived a celibate life, and spent at least half of his time in prayer and meditation. While we need not imitate Francis literally, we can understand the universal truth that he embodied: true joy and freedom have nothing to do with money, possessions, romance, status, academic degrees, or social position. Joy and freedom have everything to do with silence, prayer, surrender, service, grace, love for all creatures, and union with God. It is easy to understand why Yogananda referred to Francis as his patron saint. As all true gurus, Francis belongs to us all.

**Brother Francis, bless me
with your spirit.**

Transformation

January 13

"Take heed therefore – pray, meditate, and watch the tricks of the fickle mind to see if it is centered on God or not."
Yogananda

We all want to be happy, but are we willing to undergo the necessary transformation to experience true happiness? The price of lasting transformation is vigilance. We must resist the temptation of living our lives unconsciously, habitually, and reactively. We must choose to breathe with awareness in a gentle and prayerful manner. If we remain aware, we will sense God's subtle promptings: Does a certain action, response, or statement feel right? Will the fruit bring peace? Am I expressing a real truth or merely sharing an opinion? Are my words arising from my ego or are they bubbling up from the silence? Maintaining alertness has nothing to do with obsessing; it is a simple willingness to unite our will to God's will. God's perfect will allows us to consciously live a divine life, here and now.

God, transform me according to your holy will.

Transformation

January 14

"Seek first the kingdom of God, and everything else will be given unto you."
Jesus

God's love is free, but never cheap; therefore, transformation comes at a cost. If we are going to live from above – inspired by God's truth, beauty, and love, we must let go of what is below. For example, if we are going to experience God's love and protection, we must let go of every last ounce of victimhood and the emotional payoff it provides. We cannot feel sorry for ourselves and expect to feel God's love at the same time. Additionally, we must be ready to gracefully receive the answer to our prayers that we do not want: No. In hindsight, I am glad that God said no to most of my requests because I have discovered that God knows best. In short, when beginning any new undertaking, we must be willing to let go of our defenses and offer our efforts and energies to God, seeking only to be an instrument of God's love.

God, give me the grace to let go and the willingness to accept your plan for me.

Transformation

January 15

"Wherever two or more are gathered in my name, there am I in the midst of them."
Jesus

When I began to meditate in earnest, my teacher would often make me meditate with him. On the days we did not meet together, he required me to phone him. Words cannot express how helpful this daily contact was for me. I experienced a literal exchange of grace or energy between us which elevated my consciousness and allowed my meditation practice to deepen. Spiritual transformation can be caught from others. Yogananda said again and again, "Environment is more important than will power." We can become saints by spending time with saints and others who wish to become saints. Yes, God is present to all of us in the depth of our own souls, but God makes our transformation easier by allowing Divine Love to flow to us from others.

**God, thank you for the teachers
who give your love to me.**

Transformation

January 16

"My thoughts belong to the Holy Spirit. They are not mine."
Therese of Lisieux

When we look at the wondrous splendor and diversity of creation, we catch a glimpse of God's creative imagination. God generously shares with us the faculty of imagination, which is essential for a full and happy life. We must use imagination wisely. Uninspired imagination carries no transformative energy, and imagination captivated by darkness spawns only suffering. To use imagination wisely, we must direct it toward the inspiration of the Holy Spirit. When we nurture prayerful silence and direct our aspirations toward heaven, we allow God to use our imaginations to guide our lives and create our futures. God desires to create for us a life story based on truth, beauty, and goodness – a life story which blesses everyone. Such is the potential of imagination. Use this beautiful gift consciously.

God, let nothing inspire my imagination but your Holy Spirit.

Transformation

January 17

"We must not let ourselves fall into the vortex of pessimism. Faith can move mountains! Faith is no refuge for the faint hearted. It makes us aware of a magnificent calling, the vocation of love."
Pope Francis

If our deepest longings are to become a reality in our lives, we must have faith, which is a gift of God, yet a gift which does not come to us without effort. To open ourselves to the gift of faith, we must prayerfully and persistently direct our yearnings and needs to God and guru with heart-felt vulnerability. Most certainly, God will bless us with the gift of faith. When God gives us faith, we must protect it. We must avoid unnecessary discussions and philosophies and stay attuned to the guru. We must feed the flame of truth with meditation and silence, and we must avoid inertia. Sri Aurobindo tells us, "One must watch over one's faith as one watches over the birth of something infinitely precious."

**God, grant me the gift of faith
in your love for me.**

Transformation

January 18

"Ask and you shall receive; seek and you shall find."
Jesus

Many years ago, a spiritual director said to me: "Your ministry is beginning to make a big difference in the lives of people, but don't think that this has anything to do with your own personal strength or intelligence. It is simply the power of God bubbling up from the depths of your soul." The truth of the matter is that transformative power comes from neither the mind nor the emotions, but from the force of the Divine bubbling up from within us. When the soul fuels our actions, there is no shortage of resolve. Soul contact often begins as an intuition that we should choose a new direction. Each time we say yes to our soul's directives and take appropriate action, we grow stronger as more of the soul's light is unleashed in our lives. Begin in silence with an open heart. Then, listen to your conscience, trust your intuitions, and act accordingly. Saint Francis tells us, "Day by day and stone by stone, build your secret slowly, and you will grow to see heaven's glory."

**God, may I always be ready
for your direction.**

Trust

January 19

"God is love...His plan for creation is rooted only in love."
Yogananda

Next to the knowledge of God, nothing is more important than the knowledge of ourselves. And in order to know ourselves, we must be willing to ask some probing questions. In fact, the quality of our lives is determined by the quality of our questions, and no question is more fundamental than whether or not we trust God. If we honestly trust God, we will be consistently peaceful and content, playful, truthful, and loving. If we do not trust God we will be anxious, controlling, and self-obsessed. Either God's love is the most powerful force in creation or it is not: we cannot have it both ways. Today, act as if you trust God, regardless of whether or not you feel it. Say, "Yes, thank you, God" for every good thing that happens and "Yes, thank you, God" for every unpleasant situation.

Yes, thank you, God.

Trust

January 20

"You are a child of God. What have you to fear?"
Yogananda

Eventually, we must give up our search for God because we are never separated from God's purposeful love. As the Apostle Paul says, "We live and move and have our being in God." Accordingly, there is never an instant when God does not come forward under the guise of the present moment. If we are actually children of God, then all people and circumstances are gifts from God which serve our highest evolutionary good. If you are willing to take Jesus and Yogananda at their word, give up the impulse to complain and practice saying, "As you wish" to everything that comes to you. If you make this practice a way of life, you will experience peace, freedom, and great joy, along with the wisdom to guide you through all of life.

As you wish.

Trust

January 21

"Split the wood and I am there. Uncover the rock and I am there."
Jesus, from the Gospel of Thomas

God has taken birth in time and has been born into human history. This necessarily implies that God's great and Holy Spirit is everywhere, which means that God's love is at work at all times and in all places. The work of God's love is the expansion of our hearts so that they can hold more Divine Energy. We must avoid the temptation to tame God's love, because nothing in all of creation is as wild, demanding, and powerful. We are incapable of always knowing what God's love is creating in each and every situation. All that we need to know is that God's love is doing exactly what needs to be done in order to expand our hearts. Therefore, avoid all forms of complaining and practice silence.

**God, your love creates all
for my good.**

Trust

January 22

"My food is to do the will of the one who sent me."
Jesus

The longer I travel the spiritual path, the more I come to terms with my own limitations. This is not a form of self-disdain, but the recognition of an existential fact of the human condition: in order to really thrive, our strength and energy must come from beyond ourselves, from God. Therefore, trusting God is the spiritual food that sustains us. But trusting God does not mean that we will never experience suffering. What it does mean is that we can find strength and hope in the midst of our suffering, because God suffers with us. When you suffer, never ask why. Asking why just engages the ego and brings about even more suffering. Instead, ask for these graces: guidance, wisdom, patience, faith, and inspiration. All of these will guide you through your suffering with dignity. God loves to answer such prayers. Remember, all suffering eventually comes to an end, but God's joy is eternal!

**God, you will show me how to be
with my suffering.**

Trust

January 23

"See what you have, give it to the poor, and you will have treasure in heaven. Come, follow me."
Jesus

My spiritual director once asked me, "Do you trust God?" I answered yes. He pressed me further: "How do you know you trust God?" At that point I had no answer; I was stymied. He went on to say, "Trusting God is not first and foremost a feeling, but an action verb. It is the willingness to take risks, travel the road less taken, and be absolutely daring in the service of love." Most often, we tend to equate trust with passivity. However, trust ultimately demands action. Recently, I attended a wedding of a beautiful young couple. Clearly they trust each other, and out of that trust they are willing to build a future together. It is no different with God. If we want to create a future with God, we must trust God and be willing to take action: meditation, prayer, generosity, lifestyle changes, honesty, and use of our talents in God's service. We will discover God's trustworthiness only to the extent that we are willing to make a prayerful leap of faith.

God, help me to see the leap of faith you need me to make.

Trust

January 24

"Are you not the Mother's child? Everything is under her dispensation."
Anandamoyi Ma

Choosing to live a life of faith and trust is a most courageous decision. It will challenge our fears down to the very core of our being. Many of us have been hurt by life's apparent cruelty, sometimes very deeply. As a way of protecting ourselves, we constrict our awareness. While constricting may give us an illusion of safety, it shuts down our capacity for the experience of God's presence. In order to be radically present to God, we must make the choice to trust God's loving providence in all situations, remembering that all comes from the hand of God for our spiritual benefit. If we choose to open up we will certainly experience pain, but we will also experience union with God, which is the fulfillment of all our desires. Today, be present and trust God. What you will receive in return is priceless.

**God, open my heart
to trust in you.**

Silence

January 25

"Be still and know that I am God."
From the Jewish Psalms

Many years ago, my first spiritual director expressed a profound truth to me: "The language of God is silence, and everything else is a poor translation." Unfortunately, our culture suffers from an epidemic of noise, sensory stimulation, and information overload. The human nervous system was never meant to handle so much intense, varied input. Is it any wonder that we are plagued by a pandemic of anxiety, depression, and other stress related illnesses? Our mental and spiritual health need not be at the mercy of noise. Simple suggestions: no cell phones during meals, and no talk radio. Fast from the internet and news programming. Listen to only soothing or uplifting music and attune yourself to the sounds of nature. Spend a portion of each day in silence. Try it; I guarantee you will like it.

**God, gently draw me
into silence.**

Silence

January 26

"The kingdom of God is within you."
Jesus

Whether or not you believe in "the devil," try to stay connected to what I am about to say: the devil seldom confronts us head on. He works in crafty, indirect ways. One of his biggest ploys in the modern era is to overwhelm us with noise. Our noisy, overstimulating culture keeps us trapped in our reactive minds. The more our senses are stimulated by meaningless nonsense, instant pleasure, and emotional drama, the more we are pulled into addictive, surface-level awareness. Yet our human spirit cannot be silenced. Our spirits whisper to us in the form of dissatisfaction, low-level depression, and unsatisfied yearning. These uncomfortable feelings bid us to turn our attention within. We would do well to listen, because our deepest, noblest voice is also God's voice.

God, turn my attention inward.

Silence
January 27

"Preach the gospel, and use words only when absolutely needed."
Saint Francis of Assisi

Self-honesty is a powerful tool in the spiritual life. If we are honest with ourselves, we will readily admit that we are enamored with our own thoughts. For this reason, humility is most important in the spiritual life. In particular, the experience of spiritual silence demands humility because the thoughts produced by the reactive mind do not matter at all. Our preoccupation with our thoughts and their resulting emotions only feeds the compulsive mind. Unless our thoughts arise from a compassionate heart, they should be utterly ignored or surrendered to God. I am suggesting a form of Franciscan poverty – not material poverty, but a poverty that rejects the thinking of the habitual mind and embraces those insights which have the scent of truth and love.

**God, allow me to watch
my thinking with humility.**

Silence

January 28

"Make every yoke you accept easy and every burden you carry light."
Valentin Tomberg

People often think that meditation and the spiritual life is about wrestling the mind into silent submission. You can try that approach if you want, but it does not work. The world's saints and sages suggest a different approach: ignore the mind's machinations while placing a portion of your awareness on God in the form of a mantra, an image, or a prayer. Over time, more and more of your attention will be absorbed into God. You will then have the peace which surpasses all understanding and life will become easy and light – because God is living in and through you.

God, Christ, Guru.

Silence
January 29

"The powers of the mind are like rays of dissipated light; when they are concentrated, they illumine."
Swami Vivakananda

If we are honest with ourselves, we can admit that our will is often infatuated with something other than God – typically, a perceived pleasure. All the forces of heaven cannot make us direct our awareness to God. It must come from within us, as an act of love. Jesus tells us that the moment we turn our hearts toward God that heaven responds "in measure pressed down and overflowing." When God's dynamic will is joined with our will, we become a powerful force for good. What a wonderful way to live!

God, Christ, Guru.

The Guru

January 30

"Even though you may want to put God the Mother aside, She will not leave you. Are you not her offspring? All is under her dispensation."
Anandamayi Ma

Life on planet Earth can be beautiful but also painfully challenging. If we are going to climb through life's steep challenges with wisdom and grace, we need more than a stiff upper lip. We need reassurance and grace along the way; we need the Divine Mother. Anandamayi Ma, "Mother," who lived in India from 1896 – 1982, is another incarnation of the Divine Mother. Offering profound comfort, she tells us, "Rest assured that your worries and tribulations are ever before my eyes." I encourage you to meditate on her words and let them sink into your soul. We are not orphans. We have a Mother who watches over us with fierce love and tender compassion.

**Divine Mother,
I am your child.**

The Guru
January 31

"Verily, Ma Herself is always with you."
Anandamayi Ma

My mother was my first teacher. She taught me how to be properly human, wise, and loving. I watched how compassionately she treated people, especially those who were difficult to like. I saw how hard she worked and how she moved through life with a humble spirit. Ma tells us: "Observe truth in speech, thought, and action. Keep simplicity in food and dress. Hold a spirit of service for your parents, children, spouses, and neighbors; your services to them reach God. Ever remember that the joys and sorrows of this world are fleeting shadows of your own self. Playing with divine forces brings everlasting peace and happiness. Remember always the repetition of God's name, which has the power to wash away all karma of this life or of past lives.

**Divine Mother,
I am your child.**

Meditation

February 1

"The more you meditate, the more helpful you can be to others, and the more deeply you will be in tune with God."
Yogananda

Early on in my meditation practice I was having a particularly troublesome day. I called my meditation teacher, looking for his support and wisdom. His first response was a question: "Did you meditate today?" I told him that I had not, and he said abruptly, "Meditate, and if you need to call me afterwards, fine." After my meditation, I no longer needed to speak to him. It is impossible to have our lives centered deeply in God without a daily meditation practice. Otherwise, our innate tendencies control our lives in the form of mental, emotional, and behavioral reactivity. Meditation allows us to stand apart from our compulsions and to compassionately witness the machinations of our minds. The more we meditate, the more we realize that God is actually meditating us.

**God, grant me the joy
of the discipline of meditation.**

Meditation

February 2

"When you pray, go into your room, shut the door, and pray in secret. Then your Father who sees in secret will reward you."
Jesus

To paraphrase a question that the great Saint Teresa of Avila often asked people, "Do you meditate to have good experiences, or do you meditate because you love God?" At all costs, we must avoid spiritual consumerism, which is the tendency to collect spiritual experiences, spiritual gurus, and spiritual paths. The way of the mystic is not addition but subtraction, that is, letting go of everything we think we know and everything we have accomplished. Nature abhors a vacuum, but God is attracted to the emptiness of a humble, childlike heart. This means that we don't meditate to gain anything, but to let go of everything, most especially ourselves – so that we make room for God, who is everything.

**God, empty my heart and my head
to make room for you.**

Meditation

February 3

"Look within yourself; remember, the Infinite is within you."
Yogananda

We all suffer from a case of mistaken identity: we believe that we are ultimately the body, the personality, or the mind. These temporary structures are contained within the soul. The soul is not something we have or possess, but who we truly are. The soul, the divine image, is not the result of genetics or luck, but the very handiwork of God. At your deepest core the very flame of God's presence burns perpetually within you. Our true identity unfolds within the silence that is born of meditation, prayer, and surrender to God. In the silence, all that is not authentically you eventually falls away, and only the divine image remains. Then, our entire life becomes a living meditation, overflowing with sacred energy.

**In the silence of meditation,
may I know that I am a Soul.**

Meditation

February 4

"By contacting God first, you harness your will and activity to the right goal."
Yogananda

When I was attending a Catholic school and in the seventh grade, I was required to attend mass each morning with my classmates. One morning during mass I allowed myself to fall asleep, only to be awakened by a sharp pain in my left shoulder. The source of the pain was the hand of Sister Virginia squeezing my shoulder bone as she whispered, "Wake up; God is near" into my ear. Thankfully, suffering is not the only way to awaken from a sleepy, half-alive experience. When practiced sincerely and regularly, meditation has the power to stir us into enlightened wakefulness. Meditation takes us beneath our habitual thoughts and patterns, opening us to unimagined possibilities. Meditation reveals our God-given capacities for clarity, wisdom, freedom, and divinely inspired desire. Meditation uncovers our true humanity, simultaneously revealing our innate divinity.

**In meditation, may I discover
the divinity you share with me.**

Meditation

February 5

"By contacting God first, you harness your will and activity to the right goal."
Yogananda

Those of us who have had children or deeply loved a family member know that these dear ones are always on our minds and in our hearts. At some level, we are always radiating our love and concern for them. What is true below is also true above. Simply, it is the very nature of God to lovingly communicate with us at all times and in all places. The real question is whether or not we are listening. Without a consistent meditation practice, hearing God's voice is virtually impossible. Most of us have too much mental static and too many interior storms. Meditation calms the nervous system, stills the mind, and pacifies the heart – all essential for hearing God's voice. Meditation takes time, discipline, and commitment: the necessary cost of living a happy, inspired life.

**You speak to me at all times
and in all places.**

Perpetually in God

February 6

"We live and move and have our being in God."
Saint Paul

Human relationships truly mirror our relationship with the Divine. In a relationship that is loving and mature, we learn to see others not as objects but as people. When we truly love someone, we appreciate his or her unfolding mystery. Similarly, God is not a thing among things, a person among persons, or a god among gods. Rather, God is the Root of all Roots, the Ground of all Beings, and the Life of all Lives. Wherever we are, God is; we cannot be where God is not; we are always in God. Spirituality is not about finding God, but discovering that we are perpetually in God – we exist in an infinite sea of truth, beauty, and goodness. The spiritual life is the process whereby God softens our hearts, so that God's Is-ness is able to shine through us in brighter and brighter tones of light and love.

Wherever I am, you are.

Craig Bullock

Perpetually in God

February 7

"Knock and the door shall be opened unto you. It pleases the Father to give you the kingdom."
Jesus

Jesus described his fundamental message as "good news." The good news that Jesus proclaimed is so good that it is almost too good to be true! Authentic spirituality challenges us to believe the unbelievable. Do we dare to believe that God is pure love? That God is never disappointed in us? That we are forgiven for everything we have done and everything we will do? That the power of God's love trumps karma? That God dwells in the hearts of all people – believer or unbeliever, good or bad, rich or poor? That our souls are made to radiate God's goodness? That God makes all things work together for good? That God's Love – the most powerful force in the universe, is available to us at all times? Can we dare to believe the unbelievable? Such belief is the path of saints, sages, and all liberated souls.

**Help me to believe
what is unbelievable.**

Perpetually in God

February 8

"God is simple, and everything else is complex."
Yogananda

We human beings tend to be complicated, sometimes very complicated. A kind of civil war rages within us. We have competing desires, numerous aversions, and contradictory plans. There is no judgment in this; we cannot help it! We are complicated; God is not. We have many differing thoughts and moods; God does not. We have feelings: happy or not, loving or not. God does not. We are born; we grow; we develop; we change forms. God, though, is ever the same – because God is pure simplicity. God can only love you, because God is simple, pure Love. God can only be good to you, because God is simple, pure Goodness. While we can be many things, God can only be God – which is to say that God is simple, unchanging truth, beauty, and goodness, regardless of what we do or do not do.

**God, may I be simple
as you are simple.**

Perpetually in God

February 9

"Always remember, nothing can touch you if you inwardly love God."
Yogananda

On our wedding day, Vicki offered me her unconditional love, and I made a commitment to her that excludes any other romantic interest. God's love is absolutely free and extended to us at every moment of our existence. But we must not confuse free with cheap. In order to receive God's unbounded love, we must let go of lesser loves: attachments, desires, obsessions, compulsions, and addictions. We must be willing to leave behind superficial enjoyments for the one, ultimate enjoyment: God's love. For example, silence is the necessary price of hearing God's voice, meaning that we must let go of chattiness, gossip, and personal opinions in order to be guided by Divine Wisdom. I am not espousing misery as a spiritual path, but rather reminding you that Jesus, Francis, and Yogananda taught us that true happiness is found in loving God with all our heart, with all our soul, with all our strength, with our entire mind, and loving our neighbors as ourselves.

God, give me the willingness to let go of whatever keeps me from you.

Love

February 10

"All will know you are my disciples by your love of one another."
Jesus

Jesus and Yogananda bid us to love others. The word "love" is the most used yet the most misunderstood word in the English language. Yet it is essential to the spiritual life, so it is crucial that we have a valid understanding of what it means to love. Ultimately, it is impossible to define love, because God is love and it is impossible to define God. We know, however, how love manifests in creation: as masculine and feminine. The masculine side of love expresses itself as service – doing those things that serve others' happiness and well-being. The feminine face of love validates others' being-ness, appreciating not what they do, but who they are. If both aspects of love are not present, there is no love. If there is no love, there is no spiritual maturity.

**God, may I truly understand
the meaning of love.**

Love

February 11

"Love is God."
Sri Yukteswar

True love manifests as the willingness to serve the highest good of the other and the honoring of the other's innate goodness. Such love is not the fruit of self-esteem, ego strength, or psychological insight. Authentic love is neither self-generated nor born of our human willfulness. Love is God. Therefore, the capacity to love always flows from God. If we want to love others, we must first love God and exist in the stream of God's love. We enter into this stream in and through prayerful meditation. From a state of loving communion with God, love naturally flows from us to others. We do not love with our own love; we love with God's love. There is no such thing as my love or your love: there is only God's Love.

Only your love.

Love

February 12

"Love is the most powerful force in all of creation, and the least understood."
Pierre Teilhard de Chardin

Truly, we are hard-wired for love. But in our culture, we tend to reduce love to a feel-good emotion. While the experience of love is often accompanied with great joy, it is much more than an emotion. Love is the evolutionary energy of God working within creation to bring about our highest good. The energy of love will do whatever needs to be done in order to facilitate our growth – at times showing up as gentleness, and at other times as fierceness. We must avoid the tendency to domesticate love. Love is wild because God is wild!

**God, you will love me
as I most need to be loved.**

Love

February 13

"God is love. Every saint who has penetrated to the core of reality testifies to a divine, universal plan that is beautiful and full of joy."
Yogananda

Growing up Catholic, I was spiritually fed with stories of saints. For me, they were bigger-than-life, other-worldly figures who were impossible to emulate. Now, in the context of Kriya Yoga and the teachings of the Christian mystics, I have developed a more accurate and helpful understanding of what makes a saint a saint. Believe it or not, it has nothing to do with having a perfectly spotless personality. True saints are people who have experientially learned that God is love; thus, they have full confidence in God's goodness. They are free – to take risks and fail or succeed, to be playful and creative, to be honest and generous, to be tough or soft, to say, "I'm sorry," and to be a fool for God. Saints have gambled everything on love, goodness, and grace. Their lives demonstrate that God's love is, indeed, a sure thing.

God, I can gamble everything on you.

Love

February 14

"It is not good that Adam should be alone."
Genesis

How do we know we are in the presence of a truly loving person? The answer is simple: they see us for the person we actually are, good and bad traits alike, in a spirit of unconditional acceptance. For this reason, we must never reduce love to an emotion or a gust of romantic passion. Love takes many, many forms. All of these different loves have their roots in one loving source: God. All forms of love begin with the willingness to consciously recognize others as real people with real hopes and needs, joy and pain. We must make others as real to us as we are to ourselves. This is what Adam meant when he said of Eve, "She is bone of my bones and flesh of my flesh." Today, choose one person in your life and choose to really see him. Give him your full attention; make his needs as real as your needs. Watch him blossom and feel yourself blossoming with him. When we love others purely and generously, God literally breathes in and through us.

**God, I want to see others
as you see them.**

Love

February 15

"Love your neighbor as yourself."
Jesus

As a college student, I told my spiritual director that I needed to love myself more. He chuckled and responded, "Good luck with that." He asked me if I worried about self-esteem when I was praying, meditating, or serving. Of course, I could only answer no. Self-love is one of the most misunderstood concepts in contemporary culture. Far too often self-love has been reduced to infatuation with the personality or self-image. This kind of self-love requires an endless stream of praise, stroking, and sweet-talk from self and others, and it never really works because it is not self-love at all. Authentic self-love is not self-generated, but flows naturally when we place ourselves in God's presence so that God can mirror to us who we really are – our actual identity and our true essence. In catching a glimpse of God, we begin to experience ourselves as God's image and likeness. As such, we naturally and effortlessly radiate goodness, creativity, strength, and compassion. We become love itself.

**God, when you hold the mirror,
help me to believe what I see in it.**

Love

February 16

"On the third day there was a marriage in Cana, and the mother of Jesus was there. Jesus was also there, along with his disciples."
The Gospel of John

One of the most joyous of human experiences is a wedding celebration of two people deeply in love. On such an occasion, heavenly graces are released. It is no coincidence, therefore, that Jesus performed his first miracle at a wedding celebration, turning water into wine. This marriage celebration launched Jesus' ministry. A marriage unites two separate lives into a common life, a common trajectory, and a common destiny. Only the power of love is capable of uniting people. A good wedding overflows with the power of love. Only love can create miracles. If we want miracles in our lives we must live as if our lives are a perpetual wedding celebration which overflows with love, passion, commitment, and faith. The commitment to love unleashes the Holy Spirit, God's love, into our lives.

Your love will bring miracles into my life.

Love

February 17

"All will know you are my disciples by your love of one another."
Jesus

A number of years ago, my spiritual director challenged something in my behavior, and not in an easy-going manner. Reflexively, I told him that he was not being loving. He replied, "It is because I love you that I am telling you the truth." In our secular culture, we have reduced love to something pleasant, nice, or nonjudgmental. We have made love into something other than love. Authentic love is the power that draws creation – and us – back to God. If gentle persuasion will bring us home to God, then love will manifest as gentle persuasion. If we need to hit rock-bottom in order to go to God, then love will show up as a personal crisis. Love without truth is not love. The marriage of compassion and truth is love, and this love indeed sets us free.

**Whatever brings me
home to you is love.**

Love

February 18

"To forget God is to miss the whole point of existence. Learn to feel God and enjoy him."
Yogananda

We all want to be happy – it's a natural instinct. But what most of us don't realize is that happiness is always the fruit of something else. When we pursue happiness for the sake of happiness we typically end up feeling miserable. If we want to be happy, find peace, and experience real success, we must organize our lives around a simple, unifying purpose: the love of God. To the degree that we chase after other gods, no matter how glittery they may be, we suffer. Finding God's love does not require that we all join monasteries and do nothing but meditate, but we can all do these things: Let God be the first thought you have in the morning and the last thought you have at night. Let everything you do be for the love of God, not for the results. Love your spouse, your children, your friends and your enemies for the love of God. When all our energies are concentrated on God, our thoughts become clear and focused; our emotions, rich and steady; our will, strong and unstoppable. This is why Jesus said, "Seek first the kingdom of God, and everything else you need will be given unto you."

**May all I think, feel, and do
be for love of you.**

Love

February 19

"We live and move and have our being in God."
Saint Paul

In order for our relationships to maintain their vitality and transformative power, we must make the conscious choice to cherish the people we love. Cherishing people is the opposite of a mechanical or habitual way of interacting. To cherish our brothers and sisters is to decide to see them with fresh eyes, to consciously hold them dear during even the most ordinary of circumstances, and the determination to look beyond appearances, that is, to peer into their deepest depths. If this is true in human love, it is also true in our relationship to God. At all times and in all circumstances, we are encountering God. But do we cherish these encounters? Do we look below the surface of our lives to see that it is the Divine Life that is literally sustaining our lives, that the Spirit is the blood running through our veins, and that God is the nourishment in the food we eat? Do we understand that God's love is the benevolent and unifying energy within all human loves? Do we cherish the fact that God cherishes us? We only become conscious of God to the extent that we cherish God.

Beloved, you are the nearest of the near and the dearest of the dear.

Love

February 20

"God's plan for creation is rooted only in love."
Yogananda

What is true below is true above. For example, nature does not waste anything; everything that is will eventually be recycled into something else. Heaven works the same way! But because we are not fully evolved, we don't always understand the ways of Divine Love. God's love, the most powerful force in all of creation, works in all circumstances to expand our consciousness and to evolve us. Love uses both our successes and our failures to expand our capacity for generosity and compassion. At some point in our evolution we will understand why certain things had to happen to us and how God used them for our growth. For now, our understanding is partial at best. Until we understand fully, some form of this prayer will have to sustain us: God, I don't always understand your ways, but I believe you are the fullness of love and goodness. Do with me as you wish.

As you wish.

Love

February 21

"If you radiate love and goodwill to others, you will open the channel for God's love to come to you. Through meditation and service to mankind, you will develop Divine Love, the magnet which draws to you all good."
Yogananda

By now, I hope that you realize that Love is far more than a passionate gust of emotion. Love is literally a power which serves a singular purpose: to heal us of fear and shame and to restore us to our original innocence. However, we must realize that love does not coerce; we cannot simply wait passively for its dynamic force. God inspires our love, but we also inspire God's love, as the give and take of two lovers in an intimate dance. God needs our yes, our consent, and our participation. Today, pray earnestly, sincerely, and persistently to be a channel of God's love. Do even the simplest of tasks with great attention, devotion, and purity. Allow God to fashion you into a living expression of love.

**Make me a channel
of your peace.**

Living Spiritually

February 22

"Be as simple as you can be; you will be astonished to see how uncomplicated and happy your life can become."
Yogananda

Typically, I recommend that people on a deeply spiritual path throw away their self-help books. I say this because self-help books most often try to get us to focus our attention on perfecting our personalities. The goal of the spiritual life has nothing to do with perfecting the personality; any attempt to do so is merely another ploy of the ego and destined to create more suffering. Rather, we need the willingness to let go of the mind, releasing our tendency to judge, control, and manipulate life. Letting go, however, does not occur in a vacuum. We must let go to something greater than ourselves. The ego will only release its grip on our lives in the divine presence of God. This is why the spiritual life is the simple process of availing ourselves to God's silent, effulgent light.

**God, relieve me of
the compulsion to control.**

Living Spiritually

February 23

"Very few people know that the wholeness of God extends fully to this physical realm."
Mahavatar Babaji

Many years ago, I was bemoaning some bad luck when an intuition seemed to just descend into my awareness. It went something like this: "God cares about you but not your drama." It is good to live life with robust passion, to laugh and cry. However, we must differentiate these natural human experiences from drama, the enemy of peace. If we are honest, we will admit that drama offers us a certain level of excitement. It feels good, but in a negative and destructive way. Nothing good comes from drama at all. Drama blocks our ability to think rationally and receive God's guidance. If we believe in God's providence, if we believe that our souls are immortal, and if we believe that God is with us, there is no justifiable reason for drama – ever. The antidote to drama is faith, silence, surrender, and humor.

**God, keep me from
slipping into drama.**

Living Spiritually

February 24

"Heaven and earth shall pass away, but not my words."
Jesus

Shortly after my fiftieth birthday, I realized that I was mortal and that at some point, I would not only have to let go of my plans and projects, but I would also have to say goodbye to everyone I love. Because I don't fear death, this realization did not sadden me. But it did bring me to a clarifying awareness: time is one of the most precious gifts God has ever given us. We should not spend the remainder of our lives checking off our bucket list, but we should always remain grateful for the time we have been given. I want to use the time allotted me to know and love God, to fulfill the purposes to which God has called me, to love the people God has placed in my life, and to be fully alive. In the end, the collective moments of our lives are a gift we offer to God.

Help me to remember that how I spend my time is my gift back to you.

Craig Bullock

Living Spiritually

February 25

"Environment is more important than will power."
Yogananda

The more you open your heart to God, the more sensitive you will become. Saints, mystics, and contemplatives all have sensitive souls; you are in good company. Sensitive people are particularly open to God's grace. Likewise, they absorb the energy from others and their environments very, very easily. This is why monasteries typically have walls surrounding them: to keep as much darkness as possible at a distance. For a monk living in the world, a literal wall of safety is not possible. What is possible, however, is a wall of discrimination and discernment. Choose your activities, friends, hobbies, books, and time spent with all media with prayer, wisdom, and clear purpose. If you place yourself in sacred environments, you will become a saint.

**God, help me to guard
my sensitivity, not fight it.**

Living Spiritually

February 26

"The best way to know God is through the experience of sweetness."
Saint Bonaventure

We are innately driven towards the sweetest sweetness, which is the experience of God's love. We must be on guard against those things which mimic God's sweetness but possess no substance; though pleasing to the eye, they offer nothing to the soul. These attractions are infatuations. Infatuations can take the form of a person, a material possession, the latest guru, or the newest set of teachings. They promise instant gratification, relief from all suffering, and a utopian existence. In reality, the results are short-lived, leaving us empty and frustrated. In contrast, God's sweetness expands our capacity for love, strengthens our determination to serve, increases our endurance, and blesses us with the peace which surpasses all understanding. Do not let your awareness be seduced by anything other than God.

Only true sweetness.
Only you.

Living Spiritually

February 27

"Discern the spirits."
The Apostle John

Recently, someone asked me, "Does God speak to you?" When I answered in the affirmative, she asked, "Are you crazy?" I told her that I probably am. We are social creatures, and we are always communicating with something – Earth, air, plants, people, ideas, and emotions. And because we are essentially spiritual beings, we have the potential to communicate with spiritual beings: angels, saints, and gurus. We can also open ourselves to so-called rogue spirits with bad intentions. For this reason, the discernment of spirits is very important. Our lives take on the flavor of the energy we are digesting. The good news is that at the deepest level we are capable of communicating with the Holy Spirit. We avail ourselves of God's spirit through prayer, meditation, service, silence, and humility. When in doubt, just pray.

**God, keep me aware
of what I focus on.**

Living Spiritually

February 28

"Conscience is the door – the sole, legitimate and healthy one – to a world at least as vast and much more profound, than the world which we perceive with the senses."
Valentin Tomberg

Nothing is more human, more joyful, and more reassuring than to attune ourselves to God's voice. But if we are going to develop our capacity to attune ourselves to God's voice, we must turn away from what is noisy, pretentious, and grotesque. Then, we must be willing to nurture soft eyes, ears, and hearts so that we may learn to notice that which is subtle, refined, and whispery. In this way we increase our sensitivity to both light and darkness. My friends, I am referring to the development of conscience. Conscience has two voices: one expresses remorse about a course of action that is not in God's will; the other inspires us toward love and goodness with a corresponding sense of peace or joy. Simply, I offer you this truth: a prayerful, healthy, and well-formed conscience is the voice of God.

**Teach me to watch
and listen for your voice.**

Living Spirituality

February 29

"Words are very potent vibratory actions, affecting favorably or adversely the one who utters them and also the one to whom they are directed."
Yogananda

When God decided to create the heavens and the earth, he did not have to go into his workroom to find spare parts. He merely spoke the words, "Let there be light," and we have enjoyed light ever since. God has generously shared the gift of speech – and the creative ability to use words for good or evil – with us. With that gift comes a great responsibility. Words are an important part of the energetic vibrations which we project; they impact our lives and the lives of others. The highest, most positive use of speech begins with the willingness to offer it back to God. We should only use our speech as an instrument of truth, beauty, and love. When we consistently and prayerfully place our capacity for speech at the feet of God, the power of heaven itself propels our words.

**Take my words and use them
as your own.**

Into the Wilderness

March 1

"I sacrificed everything, all attachment and delusion, to learn at last that I am in love with Love – with God."
Yogananda

It is good that we experience different seasons, because changing seasons open us to new perceptions. In the Christian tradition, Lent is a very powerful season because it taps into our innate desire for God. We have not been created for ourselves, but for God. Jesus followed his desire for union with God into the wilderness for forty days of solitude, prayer, meditation, and fasting. If we are going to give ourselves over to God, we must follow Jesus into the wilderness, not to punish ourselves, but as a way of becoming love. The goal of the spiritual life is to love – not feebly, but fiercely.

**Guruji, come with me
into the wilderness.**

Into the Wilderness

March 2

"The wonder of man's relationship with his Heavenly Father is that he does not even have to acquire God. He has him already. As soon as the veil of delusion is pulled away, he knows instantly that God is with him."
Yogananda

Saints tells us that looking for God is like a fish looking for water. This means that we are already in God and God is already in us. We exist in an ocean of bliss, joy, and love! The problem is that we objectify God, making the Divine into something we can control, possess, or chase after. The journey into the wilderness is about giving up the search for happiness, for a God that we can grasp with our minds. Wilderness consciousness is the willingness to let go of what we think we know about God. In this way, we can be present to the ever-present presence; we can breathe in God and God can breathe in us. There is only one way to know God, and it is called Love.

**I am thine
and thou art mine.**

Into the Wilderness

March 3

"Temptation is the ladder by which we ascend to God."
Saint Francis of Assisi

Without temptation and resistance, there is no growth. In the wilderness, we encounter all of our possibilities, good and bad. The journey to God-realization necessitates such encounters; we cannot avoid them. Little by little, we learn to say no to those destructive elements in our personality and yes to the God oriented tendencies which pulsate within us. With each no and each yes we become a bit more God-like, which is the very reason God loved us into existence. I am not saying that you must perfect your personality or work to earn God's love. Rather, understand that we grow into the divine likeness by free acts of truth, goodness, and love. Each choice we make for God literally increases the momentum of Divine Energy flowing within us.

**God, may you inspire
my choices today.**

Craig Bullock

Into the Wilderness

March 4

"When Francis was alone with God, he would fill the groves with sighs, sprinkle the ground with tears, strike his breasts with his fist, and, having found his secret hiding place, converse with his Lord."
Saint Bonaventure

God's truth always exceeds the grasp of our thoughts and also brings unexpected opportunities that transcend the capacity of human imagination. Wilderness is the portal into our divine possibilities. The willingness to enter into the wilderness is actually a form of spiritual poverty. In such a context, we do not have the typical distractions which occupy our attention. Our normal comforts fail us – even the comfort of our own thinking. We are alone with ourselves and God. This type of interior poverty prepares us to receive that which is new, marvelous, unexpected, and necessary from the hand of God. Spiritual poverty gives God permission to be wildly generous towards us.

**Your truth always surpasses
my thinking.**

Temptation

March 5

"The devil left Jesus, and behold, angels came no to minister unto him."
The Gospel of Matthew

At one time I complained to my spiritual director about temptations that I was experiencing. I was shocked when he said, "Stop complaining. Temptations are necessary for your growth. By resisting them, you will become spiritually strong." In the wilderness, Jesus confronted the primordial temptations common to all people. Interestingly, the angels came to him only after the temptations had ended. Temptation is never about what is happening to us, but within us. The essence of temptation is inner conflict – storms of competing desires, contradictory inclinations, and opposing forces which create stormy minds, hearts, and spirits within us. Our inner storms block the influx of spiritual energy. Jesus had to give a clear no to the tempest-like forces pulling on him. Like Jesus, we will be thrown into the storms of our own desires. By God's grace, we must learn to say no to those forces which threaten our conscious contact with God. When based in prayerful wisdom and love, the word no is a sacred and liberating spiritual practice.

**With your grace,
I will practice saying no.**

Fasting

March 6

"This kind of evil can only be driven out by prayer and fasting."
Jesus

Faith is much more than mere belief. Faith is nothing other than the all-powerful breath of God, which is capable of moving mountains, moving in us and through us. But we must avail ourselves of this gift. Otherwise, the octopus-like grip of habit, addiction, and fear will continue to rule our lives. The bottom line is this: the strength of our faith must be at least equal to the size of the mountain we are trying to move. Only intense and ardent prayer, along with the commitment to fast from our compulsions, can release the power of faith which lies within us. Today, choose to fast from a particular attachment. Then, pray for yourself or someone else with all the sincerity you can muster. Watch your faith grow and empower you.

**What attachment would you
have me fast from today?**

Fasting
March 7

"While nature abhors a vacuum, heaven is drawn to one."
Valentin Tomberg

We have been created to experience the highest happiness, and nothing short of the highest happiness will satisfy our soul's hunger. Pleasure is not bad. In fact, God desires that we experience multiple levels of pleasure. But if we are not sufficiently grounded in God's love, we make pleasure into a god. Prayer and meditation put us into conscious contact with God, the only source of a truly happy life. Once we have a taste of the superior bliss of God's presence, we recognize the limitations of all other pleasures. While recognition of our attachments is essential, recognition alone is not enough. While relying on God's grace, we must also make a conscious decision to let go of compulsive pleasures. We will fail, yet each time we try a certain emptiness opens up within our spirits which allows God's Spirit to rush into us, filling us with everything we need to live a full, creative, and joyful life.

**God, help me to see
and to let go.**

Fasting

March 8

"My food is to do the will of the Father who sent me."
Jesus

Once upon a time I loved theological debate. Then I was blessed to meet a direct disciple of Yogananda. The more philosophical questions I posed to him, the more silent he became. Finally, I got the message, and I began to fast from my complicated questions. The serious spiritual devotee makes fasting a way of life. We start by fasting from the things which cause us to suffer: addictions, compulsions, self-hatred, distortions, perfectionism, and others. Perpetual fasting is the ongoing process of renouncing our personal opinions so that we can avail ourselves of God's liberating truth. In letting go of our attachments, we receive heavenly riches. In letting go of our missions, we become available for God's mission, which is always preferable to what we can concoct for ourselves. Such fasting creates an ever-expanding spaciousness within us, allowing our bodies, minds, and spirits to become a dwelling place for God's loving presence, the very essence of joy and peace.

**In letting go,
I will receive.**

Fasting
March 9

"Fasting has been practiced by devotees of every religion since ancient times as an effective means of approaching God, a form of austerity to help bring the willful body and mind under control to receive the Spirit of God."
Yogananda

Weeds are always a danger to health, growth, and life, especially the weeds of distorted thoughts and misguided desires. Every gardener knows that it is not enough to prepare the soil, plant the seed, and provide sufficient water. Something else is needed: the garden must be weeded, or the weeds will choke the life out of what we want to grow. Distorted desires, compulsions, opinions, habits, and beliefs are weeds in the spiritual life; they block our capacity to receive God's love. Fasting is a form of spiritual weeding. Today, choose something to fast from: food, television, cable news, gossip, excessive talking, political opinions, your cell phone, anger, self-pity, or harsh judgment of yourself or others. Then, replace that weed with prayer, meditation, service, gratitude, silence, spiritual reading, nature, or laughter, filling yourself up with God.

With your help, may I lovingly weed my garden.

Fasting

March 10

"Sell what you have, give it to the poor, and come follow me."
Jesus

Just before I married Vicki, a monk reminded me that for the householder, a form of renunciation is generosity. We have all been blessed with talents, time, and treasure, gifts which come from and belong to God. While we are free to personally enjoy these blessings, they are not meant for us alone. Everything we have is to be placed at God's feet, furthering God's work and serving those in need. As we selflessly give our gifts away, something magical occurs: we open ourselves to the currency of God's goodness and grace. What we give away increases "in measure pressed down and overflowing," according to Jesus. Today, wisely spend your gifts in the service of God's purposes and those who are in need. This is real fasting!

**My God, show me what
to give away for your sake.**

Silence

March 11

"I am the resurrection and the life: he that believes in me, though he was dead, yet shall live."
Jesus

We all know that we are asleep to some extent. We know that something is missing, something is wrong, that there is more to life than we are experiencing. Many of us spend enormous amounts of energy, time, and money trying to resolve our inner angst without realizing any results. We see no results because we cannot resurrect ourselves from our own sleepiness. Only Divinity can help awaken us to the presence of the Divine. I suggest that we throw away our self-help books, let go of the impulse to fix ourselves, and simply turn our heart's attention to the guru in silence, prayer, and obedience to the divine will. God's light and love will resurrect us to our full potential.

Only you can wake me.

Silence

March 12

"Everything exposed by the light becomes visible, for everything that becomes visible is light."
Saint Paul

Yes, it is essential to bring silence into our thoughts, words, and actions. Yet even when we feel the peace of the silence, unconscious drives and longings may remain deep under the surface. We must patiently wait while we allow God's silence to penetrate and purify even the unconscious mind. The waiting requires grace from God and willingness, courage, and humility from us. As our unconscious motivations such as fear, anger, or the need to control arise, we must remain prayerfully present and surrender everything to God. If we can remain present, these unconscious drives will assert less and less influence over us and God's peaceful silence will resonate on all levels of our being. God removes all obstacles so that we may be naked before God and God may be naked before us.

**Wait with me
in the silence.**

Silence

March 13

"This zone of silence being once established, you can draw from it for both rest and for work."
Valentin Tomberg

Bringing silence into all our activities begins by introducing silence into our speech. Compulsive speaking and unconscious chatter dissipates the silence, creating all manner of distortion and confusion. We permeate our speech with silence by remaining awake and prayerful, ever conscious of our calling to be an instrument of God's wisdom and love in any and all situations. When in doubt, breathe, pray, and listen. If your words will carry the scent of truth, beauty, and goodness, then speak. If not, remain quiet. I am not asking you to be sullen or somber! The ability to make people laugh, for example, is a great blessing. Words which bubble up from the silence radiate joy, peace, and strength to one and all – because they are God's words.

**If my words are not your words,
I shall not speak.**

Silence

March 14

"What you experience in meditation, bring into your activities."
Yogananda

In the deepest silence, we experience nothing other than simple, sublime unity with God. Yet we cannot always remain in this pure bliss. We have God-given duties and responsibilities to fulfill. For the contemplative, contact with God is not reserved for meditation only, but must be integrated into all aspects of life, so that all of life can be illumined by God's wisdom and love. While the eyes of the body are involved with matters pertaining to the physical world, the eye of the soul must be turned toward God. In this way, we fulfill our true vocation, which is to be the living, breathing marriage of heaven and earth.

**May my silence bless
your entire world.**

Silence

March 15

"A true lover of God can inspire his brothers and sisters with a desire to return to their home in him; but they themselves, step-by-step, must make the actual journey."
Yogananda

Silence is the language of God and everything else is a poor translation. Entering into the silence, though, implies a degree of solitude. I am not suggesting that everyone should run away to a hermitage. What I am stating very clearly is that we need to carve out space and time to be alone with God and ourselves – even if only for twenty or thirty minutes a day. If we are willing to make this commitment, we will find our attunement with God deepening, providing us with psychological and spiritual sustenance – the Bread of Heaven.

Oh my guru, come to me.

Silence

March 16

"Jesus took James, John, and Peter up the mountain to pray."
The Gospel of Matthew

God always makes the first move, and we call that first move grace. Recently, I made plans to visit a friend in another state. When I arrived at the airport, my flight was cancelled. When I arrived the next morning, that flight was cancelled too. God had other plans for me. I spent the next few days meditating and tending to my garden. We all lead busy lives, an unintended consequence of modernity. Thus, finding time for solitude and deep, meditative silence is not easy, but it is absolutely essential. Yes, we can pray on the run, but praying on the run is never a substitute for the experience of silent, ever-expanding communion with God. We must be willing to give God a portion of our time, which is a way of being generous to God. When we are generous to God, God will be infinitely more generous with us. In truth, the solutions to all of our problems and challenges are found in silence.

Wait with me in the silence.

The Past
March 17

"When you have learned to be happy in the present, you have found the right path to God."
Yogananda

Some of us have an attachment to remaining in our past, imprisoned in regret and remorse. Of course we should learn from the past and make amends when necessary. But we should never live in the past, especially in those memories which do nothing but induce guilt and shame. One of the things we can let go of are the failings and foibles rooted in our memories. Letting go of the past is not easy; in fact, apart from God, it is impossible. But when we pray and meditate, we allow the gravitational pull of heaven to elevate us out of the past, out of our mental ruts and ingrained emotional patterns. Only God's love can break our karmic habits and set us free to live completely and joyously in the present.

God, I trust you with my past and my memories.

Shame

March 18

"God is ever-new joy."
Yogananda

In the wilderness, we practice letting go of those behaviors and attitudes which produce misery. One of the greatest sources of our unhappiness is self-consciousness, often experienced as self-contempt. Most people struggle with a sense of profound inadequacy, unworthiness, and shame. But in reality, we have been created to be God-conscious, not self-conscious: we have been fashioned to behold and reflect the absolute goodness and beauty of God. As we practice gazing at God, we naturally become less self-conscious. Our perceptions, emotions, and attitudes gradually expand as we reflect more and more of God's incomprehensible light.

God, let me never be ashamed of what you have created.

The Body
March 19

"Man shall not live by bread alone, but by every word that proceeds out of the mouth of God."
Jesus

The body is God's base of operation in the world; it supports our meditations and spiritual practices. We must learn to open our bodies to soul-force, to cosmic energy, so as to receive strength against illness and fatigue. Kriya Yoga infuses the body with soul force – as does steady breathing, correct posture, and chanting Aum (Om) through the chakras. Receiving Holy Communion with an open heart also infuses the body with soul-force. Prayer, acts of compassion, and even the choice to be happy and constructive also serve to open us to soul-force. Yogananda tells us, "A strong joyful soul makes the mind indomitably positive; such a powerful mentality in turn can influence a disease-stricken body to manifest healing and vitality."

God, my body is in your care.

The Body

March 20

"The body is a temple of the Holy Spirit."
Saint Paul

Generally speaking, people make two mistakes when it comes to the body: either they treat it with contempt or they worship it as a deity. As the body is a gift of God, a wise spiritual practice is a commitment to care for it. Caring for the body is not complicated at all. Be sure to give the body adequate rest, balancing work and recreation. Don't eat too much or too little. Stay away from red meat, pork, alcohol, marijuana, and refined sugars, and try your best to eat wholesome, organic foods. A regular routine of exercise, gently done, helps to keep the body vital, and a vital body makes for easier meditations. As we get older, it is more important to stretch the body, which also helps to stretch our souls. The goal of a healthy spiritual practice is not to deny the body, but to care for it and offer it back to God.

**May I care for my body
for your sake and mine.**

The Body
March 21

"This body of ours is a symbol of our real being."
Sri Aurobindo

We do not come to God as angels, but as human beings. We must embrace our bodies with love. Our bodies are meant to be instruments of divine energy, wisdom, and love. Therefore, we must not allow the body to impose limits on what God wants to do with us. The Holy Spirit will channel our bodily impulses and energies toward a higher purpose. God wants our bodies to reach such a level of development that they can hold as much divinity, grace, and energy as possible without wasting it or breaking down. Saint Bonaventure writes, "Francis had reached such purity that his body was in remarkable harmony with his spirit, and his spirit with God. As a result God ordained that creation should be subject in an extraordinary way to Francis' will and command."

**God, help me to love this body,
which you have given to me.**

Craig Bullock

The Illusion of Separation

March 22

"Abandoning the vain idea of a separate existence, man obtains the state of final release – oneness with the Spirit."
Sri Yukteswar

Only great saints and mystics see reality as it really is. Most of us see life through a very distorted lens. Specifically, we see and experience ourselves as separate entities, divorced from God and others. This false sense of separation is a source of great anxiety and suffering, because it creates an exaggerated sense of self-sufficiency. We have not been created to handle the extreme challenges of life by ourselves, apart from God. We live in dynamic partnership with God; there is no other way to be fully human, alive, and happy. To shed another burden in the wilderness, give up the illusion of separateness and seek to live in conscious communion with God through prayer, meditation, and selfless service.

**May I give up the idea
that I live this life alone.**

Remember

March 23

"Now a certain man was sick, named Lazarus, of Bethany, the town of Mary and her sister Martha. His sisters sent to Jesus, saying, 'Lord, behold, he whom you love is sick.'"
The Gospel of John

The sacrifices associated with the spiritual life in general serve one ultimate purpose: the resurrection of the Divine Image and Likeness within us. The fundamental sickness that we all undergo is forgetfulness. We have forgotten who we really are, and we forget that we have forgotten. Thus, we suffer. No matter how much we forget God, God always remembers us. God's unfailing remembrance of us is actually God loving us. God's love is not a sentimental affair, but the most powerful force in all of creation. The whole of human history, as well as our personal histories, is the story of God's love attempting to rouse us from our sleepy forgetfulness so that we can move from a place of suffering to a loving and joyful existence.

May I remember who I really am.

Lazarus

March 24

"Jesus was troubled in spirit...Jesus wept...Jesus groaned in his spirit...Jesus lifted his eyes toward heaven."
The Gospel of John

Some of my most profound moments of prayer happened not when I was peaceful and quiet, but when I was challenged to my core. This is why I love the story of Jesus and his friend Lazarus. Jesus' mission to raise his friend Lazarus from the dead challenged him. This was not only a physical resurrection, but a spiritual one – resurrecting Lazarus' highest, most divine possibilities. Jesus' task was daunting, to say the least. He turned to a power greater than himself, to God. He prayed from the deepest depths of his spirit with absolute sincerity. This is the meaning of Jesus' weeping and groaning. We are never more prayerfully sincere than when we are weeping and groaning. Such prayers have the power to stir heaven on our behalf and to raise the dead. May we all learn to pray as Jesus prayed, because the world needs it.

Lord Jesus, teach me to pray.

Lazarus

March 25

"Lazarus, come forth."
The Gospel of John

Often we miss the fact that Lazarus played a key role in the story of his resurrection from the dead. Lazarus, a disciple of Jesus, undoubtedly entered a state of profound rest upon his death, no longer concerned with the cares and concerns of this life. Jesus could not force Lazarus to return. So why did he? The answer to this question is simple: love. Peaceful repose is wonderful, but it cannot hold a candle to the power of love. Ultimately, we were not created for peace, but for love. Whether we are talking about Lazarus or ourselves, we will only let go of our pleasurable and safe attachments in the face of love. In the wilderness, we listen intensely to the call of Divine Love to give ourselves over to the most challenging and fulfilling life imaginable – to God, to Christ, to guru, to one another.

**God created me of love,
for love.**

Moses

March 26

"The Lord said, 'I have seen the affliction of my people and have heard their cry because of their taskmasters. I know their sufferings, and I have come to deliver them out of the hand of the Egyptians.'"
The Book of Exodus

What is the ultimate sign of one's spiritual growth? Moses led his people out of slavery, through the wilderness, and into the Promised Land. The ultimate verification of an actual encounter with God is not personal happiness, but the capacity to be a source of peace, love, and liberation for others. God is not the God of the Jews or the Christians or the Hindus or the Muslims, but the God of all people. Neither is God merely a happy feeling, but the evolutionary and unifying power of love. Everyone is lovingly embraced by God. Thus, to the extent that one is truly caught up in God, he or she becomes like God – able to embrace all people and be of service to them. Jesus said, "All men will know that you are my disciples by your love for one another."

**May I be a servant of all
and a lover of all.**

Moses

March 27

"Now Moses came to Horeb, the mountain of God."
The Book of Genesis

Ultimately, the time we spend in the wilderness serves only one purpose: to prepare us for an encounter with God. The story of Moses' experience on Mount Horeb is not only an encounter with God, but a timeless, universal blueprint for the blessed meeting between God and humankind. Like us, Moses was not a saint. In fact, he was a man on the run, wanted in Egypt for murder. This tells us that the encounter with God has nothing to do with our being good enough; it is always predicated on God's grace, goodness, and generosity. What matters most is not the past, but the present moment – wherein God is fully present, loving us and calling to us.

**I wait for you in the wilderness,
just as I am.**

Craig Bullock

The Last Supper

March 28

"I am the Bread of Life."
Jesus

Christians commemorate the Last Supper of Jesus with his disciples at this time of year. Fully aware of his imminent death, Jesus observed the Passover meal by breaking bread with his dearest friends. Not only was the bread broken, but the very heart of Jesus broke open, spilling out his love, compassion, and consolation. The lesson for us is clear. In order to come through the wilderness we must pass through our own hearts. We must be vulnerable, setting aside our self-protective schemes and acknowledging our need for God. Self-help strategies will not help us at this time – only love can. Today, let your heart be vulnerable. Be real. Laugh, weep, love, and serve. At the deepest level, our hearts and God's heart are one and the same.

Let my heart be your heart.

The Passion of Jesus
March 29

"Father forgive them, for they know not what they do."
Jesus

We are all possessed by unconscious fears, drives, and impulses. Even though we cause others and ourselves to suffer, we almost never do so consciously. Jesus understood human nature! This is why he prayed while on the cross, "Father forgive them, for they know not what they do." Jesus came to stir us into wakefulness, to illumine our minds, and to enlighten our hearts so that our choices would become lovingly conscious, wisely purposeful, and compassionately creative. Jesus knew that condemning us would only drive us into hiding, into deeper levels of defensiveness and more unconsciously destructive behavior. Therefore, at his darkest moment he gave us what we needed most: mercy, forgiveness, and grace, because only in the presence of great love are we capable of diving into our own souls. As you read these words, consider the possibility that you are forgiven for everything you have done, are doing, and will do. God is at peace with you; now be at peace with yourself.

Father, forgive me. I am powerless and my life is unmanageable.

Craig Bullock

The Passion of Jesus

March 30

"Father, if you are willing, remove this cup from me. Nevertheless, not my will but thy will be done."
Jesus

If we willingly remain in the wilderness with Jesus' death, we too will experience a death of sorts: the death of our own willful agenda. If in coming out of the wilderness we are the same person who began the journey, we really have not made the journey at all. The closer we are to union with God, the more our own cleverness, strategies, and energies fail us. At a certain point we must let go of ourselves into God, into Love. This will feel like a death because it is the death of the ego-self, the illusion of separateness, and fear. When we reach this threshold, we have no choice but to pray as Jesus prayed: "Not my will, but Thy will be done." We must not forget, however, that immediately after Jesus prayed his prayer of surrender, we are told that "An angel of heaven appeared to strengthen him." What was true for Jesus is true for us. When we attune our will to God's will, heaven floods us with grace, wisdom, and angelic blessings.

**Not my will,
but Thy will be done.**

The Passion of Jesus

March 31

"Jesus yielded his spirit. And behold, the curtain of the temple was torn in two."
The Gospel of Matthew 27: 50-51

Jesus' last words were, "It is finished." He had finished the work that God had given him: to bring humanity into conscious communion with God's loving presence. The temple curtain being torn in two symbolizes the completion of Jesus' work: now everyone, not just the temple priests, would have access to God's abundance. Through recognition of Jesus' mission, we realize that Jesus' life was not about himself, but about his service to God and us. In Jesus we see a fundamental spiritual truth in action: what is above serves that which is below. Gurus serve their disciples; angels serve us; heaven serves earth; and ultimately, God serves us all. Therefore, if we want to be in the flow of God's truth, beauty and goodness, we have no choice but to spend our lives serving God and one another. The fruit of such service is the resurrection of our full potential as human beings who are created in the Divine Image. There is no other path to freedom!

Beloved guru, can I dare to believe that you and all of heaven serve me?

Craig Bullock

Waiting in Darkness

April 1

"It was by sheer grace for the soul that God brought it into this dark night, from whence such great good came to it, and into which it would never have been able to enter by itself. Besides, no one would be capable through his own forces alone of disengaging himself from all his tendencies in order to go forth to God."
Saint John of the Cross

Jesus' body laid lifeless in a darkened tomb, his mission apparently dead and his despairing disciples hiding in the shadows. Yet, something was happening, hidden from the human eye. In the midst of this murky darkness, God was at work divinizing every aspect of Jesus' humanity. Before we can be resurrected, we will all enter into our own experience of the dark night. This experience is neither a punishment nor an abandonment. We are never closer to resurrection than when God lovingly darkens our minds, senses, and will.

**When all I can see is darkness,
you work in my life.**

Waiting in Darkness

April 2

"Now Mary Magdalene and another Mary kept vigil there, seated opposite the tomb."
The Gospel of Matthew

Every legitimate contemplative path underscores the necessity of wakeful alertness. Waiting in darkness means:

- Sitting in silence and love
- Sitting with trusted spiritual friends
- Not needing instant gratification
- Seeking the Beloved, not answers
- Willingness to hold onto hope
- Waiting as long as necessary
- Patiently tolerating uncertainty
- Silence without meaningless discussion
- Allowing outcomes to unfold without force
- Total reliance on grace and God's goodness

Today's reflection was inspired by the writings of Richard Rohr, my spiritual mentor.

Wait with me.

Resurrection

April 3

"I am the resurrection and the life. He who believes in me, even should he die, shall live."
Jesus

God's love did what medicine, science, and technology will never be able to do: it transformed Jesus' dead body into a living, breathing fountain of Divine Life. The most influential force in creation is not fear, the lust for power, or the pull of addiction. It is God's Love. Despite the presence of darkness in the world, we need never be afraid. We are free to embrace today, tomorrow, and the entire future fearlessly. Each time we pray, meditate, open our eyes to beauty, or touch someone who suffers, we avail ourselves of the very same love that raised Jesus from the dead. To be a spiritual person is to carry resurrection within our hearts and to become fountains of Divine Love. Be at peace.

Resurrection is ever before me.

Resurrection

April 4

"I am the resurrection and the life. He who believes in me, even should he die, shall live."
Jesus

God's love did what medicine, science, and technology will never be able to do: it transformed Jesus' dead body into a living, breathing fountain of Divine Life. The most influential force in creation is not fear, the lust for power, or the pull of addiction. It is God's Love. Despite the presence of darkness in the world, we need never be afraid. We are free to embrace today, tomorrow, and the entire future fearlessly. Each time we pray, meditate, open our eyes to beauty, or touch someone who suffers, we avail ourselves of the very same love that raised Jesus from the dead. To be a spiritual person is to carry resurrection within our hearts and to become fountains of Divine Love. Be at peace.

Resurrection is ever before me.

Resurrection

April 5

"Across the immensity of time, one single thing is being made: the mystical body of Christ."
Teilhard de Chardin

The resurrection of Jesus is not meant to be a remote, distant-past experience that we worship from afar. We are meant to experience Jesus' resurrection here and now. What we don't realize is that the very same grace that divinized Jesus' dead body is at work in our own lives. Every time we are inspired to forgive, to love, to transcend a limitation, or to surrender to God's will, we are being moved by the exact Divine Energy which transformed Jesus. The difference is only a matter of degree. Every time we enter into silence, pray, or seek to be an instrument of God's love, the divine spark within us burns brighter and brighter. This is the heart and soul of the resurrection experience.

**That which resurrected Jesus
resurrects me.**

Resurrection
April 6

"Read a little, meditate more, and think of God always."
Yogananda

How do we allow God's light and love to resurrect our own lives? I hope the following suggestions will help.

- Begin each day in prayerful silence. Without silence, there is no meditation!
- Ask God for help and guidance. God loves to answer such prayers.
- Don't try to perfect yourself.
- Always surrender your pain and confusion to God.
- Look people in the eye when you talk to them – and bless them.
- Ignore the temptation to blame self and others.
- Ignore old critical voices.
- Express gratitude for everything, even your biggest challenges.
- Do everything for the love of God, even the most mundane tasks.
- Get enough rest. Laugh, play, and don't take yourself too seriously.

God, may my life allow room for resurrection.

God's Loving Providence

April 7

"Not even a lowly sparrow falls to the ground without the Father's knowledge."
Jesus

One of the most radical truths that Jesus and Yogananda put forth was that of God's loving providence. Our minds will never be able to completely make sense of this truth. Our hearts, however, can intuitively grasp the fullness of God's love, enabling us to rest in God's goodness. Whether life is easy or hard, pleasant or painful, sensible or confusing, we always exist in the center of God's loving providence, and all our experiences serve our highest good. We can relax and rest. The medieval Catholic mystic Julian of Norwich tells us, "All is well, all shall be well, and all manner of things shall be well."

**Divine Mother, touch my heart
that I may know how you care for me.**

God's Loving Providence

April 8

"The man who has peace in his soul has all the wisdom of the gods."
Yogananda

I must be honest. In my spiritual journey, I have hoped that God would bring me to the Promised Land through a path of great glory. I have experienced moments of keen illumination, for which I am most grateful. What I really wanted, though, was release from suffering – and not God. By grace and the guru's guidance, I finally realized that God's will is preferable to anything I might otherwise desire. God's will brought me everything I was looking for: love, wisdom, and peace. Of course, surrender to God's will is a process, not a destination. But to the extent that we surrender to Divine Providence, we are restored to our innate dignity in God. A wise monk once told me, "Living to please God is the only way to live."

**Your will brings me
love, wisdom, and peace.**

Craig Bullock

God's Loving Providence

April 9

"What God arranges for us to experience in each moment is the best and holiest thing that could happen to us."
Jean-Pierre De Cussade

Whether we realize it or not or whether we want to believe it or not, we are inseparable from God. We must always remember that God dwells in the very center of the human drama as a loving, organizing, and transforming presence. John's gospel tells us, "The Word was made flesh and dwelt among us." God abides not only in the great cathedrals of the world, but in the nooks and crannies of our lives. God has penetrated into the heart of humanity so as to gather us – exactly as we are – into the Divine Life. Only when we accept with faith all that God offers to us moment by moment will we become truly, deeply peaceful.

**Moment by moment,
you offer me peace.**

God's Loving Providence

April 10

"The very hairs on your head are known and numbered."
Jesus

The path to freedom has nothing to do with a strange or esoteric secret. Rather, it is all about becoming childlike. In the context of God's loving and purposeful will, the secret is to resist nothing and accept everything. This is not an invitation to passivity or victimhood. Rather, it is an acknowledgment that God is present in all circumstances and events, most especially in our suffering. If God is present, then the seeds of providence and redemption are also present. Acceptance empowers us to stand back from fear, anxiety, and anger, giving us the space to breathe, pray, and listen to the voice of God. Thus, we don't react; we respond, with the wisdom and strength of heaven behind us.

**God, help me resist nothing
and accept everything.**

God's Loving Providence

April 11

"A kitten is carried about by the mother cat, content wherever she places her. I am like that; I give all responsibility to the Divine Mother. But to maintain that attitude takes great will."
Yogananda

If we dive deep enough into the spiritual life, really living for God, we grow more and more awake. As a result, we experience more light, joy, and goodness than we ever could have imagined. Conversely, our capacity for pain also expands. Often this paradox leads us to a crossroads of sorts: either we yield to despair, or we ask for the grace to surrender entirely to God and guru, accepting the truth that we are kittens being carried about by the Divine Mother. Then, as Yogananda writes, "You have faith that She knows best." Ultimately, we let go. A peace, grounding, and wisdom arise within us, but it is clearly not from us. Our little life is giving way to a larger, Divine Life.

Place me where you wish,
and may I remain content.

The Guru
April 12

"The masters or shepherds of this world come down from their high places and give their lives searching for disciples who are lost in darkness."
Yogananda

God's voice always resonates in and through creation, attempting to lovingly guide our lives towards greater wholeness and freedom. However, most of us do not know how to hear God's voice – not because we are bad people, but because no one has ever taught us to do so. So, God sends us masters, saints, and avatars who embody the Divine voice, so that we can hear and understand it.

Attuning ourselves to God's voice begins with the willingness to sit at the feet of a God-realized saint and prayerfully reflect on his or her words. When we meditate on the words of Jesus in the New Testament, the wisdom of Krishna in the Bhagavad Gita, or the writings of Yogananda, we avail ourselves of the words of God. For a happier, more peaceful life, all we have to do is spend fifteen minutes a day silently feasting on the words of a true saint. It is that simple!

Oh my guru, come to me.

The Guru

April 13

"I tell you, there is joy before the angels of God over one sinner who repents."
Jesus

As humans, we are social creatures, and we thrive when our relationships are harmonious, positive, and supportive. When we follow God's shepherds, God draws us into intimate communion with the heavenly realm: with saints, angels, and gurus. We become part of a visible and invisible spiritual family; we never again walk alone. Jesus love is available to us as is Francis' joy; Yogananda's strength; Sri Yukteswar's wisdom; and Divine Mother's compassion. This is more than religious sentimentality; it is reality. The only way to bring transformation into our personal and collective lives is to draw on a power greater than ourselves – the power of God, in and through God's saints and shepherds.

**God, thank you for sending
your gurus and saints.**

The Guru

April 14

"If you have seen me you have seen the Father, for the Father and I are one."
Jesus

None of us see the world or others as they really are; we don't even see ourselves as we really are because our minds are clouded by prejudice, desire, and fear. For this reason, we all need a true guru who is literally an embodiment of Divine Light. When we enter into discipleship with a guru, we allow his or her light to penetrate our awareness, thus burning away the darkness that has clouded our minds. At first, the brightness of the guru's light tends to cause discomfort. In time, though, it liberates us from illusion and suffering. Yogananda said, "The disciple is one who accepts the master's teachings wholly, with open heart and mind. He does not have to be coaxed, but follows through his own will and determination."

**My guru, bring me
from darkness into light.**

The Guru

April 15

"To fall in love with God is the greatest romance; to seek Him is the greatest adventure; to find Him is the greatest human achievement."
Saint Augustine

Jesus never said, "Worship me." He did say, "Follow me." The Buddha, Jesus, Yogananda, Anandamayi Ma – the great ones always want to take us to God, not to themselves. God does not have grandchildren, only children. We are all capable of experiencing God directly, immediately, and permanently. In fact, we will never be fully content or whole until we experience absolute oneness with God, because our DNA is divine. We come from God, and only God can satisfy the deepest desires of our hearts.

**Beloved God, you are my greatest love,
my greatest adventure,
and my greatest achievement.**

The Guru
April 16

"My sheep hear my voice. I know them, and they follow me."
Jesus

If we are honest with ourselves, we will acknowledge our capacity for self-deception. Many of us fall into the trap of projecting onto God our own notions of Divinity, effectively creating God in our own image. In the person of a guru, however, God becomes visible, concrete, and very real. While a vague, impersonal notion of God neither inspires nor challenges us, the guru inflames us with the fire of God's love and elevates us to our highest potential. No matter who your guru is, never take him or her for granted. Let the light of the gurus be the guiding vision for your life; let their words be the truth that makes straight your path; and let their grace be the bread that sustains you. When you open your heart to the guru, you are opening your soul to God!

God, thank you for my guru.

The Present Moment

April 17

"It is heaven all the way to heaven."
Saint Catherine of Genoa

Heaven is not a geographical destination, but a state of consciousness. Heaven is conscious contact with God. The good news is that it is possible to be in conscious contact with God at all times. Just stay present and alert; don't drift into sleepiness or dullness. Stay present and alert; don't run to the past or flee to the future. Stay present and alert; don't avoid discomfort and don't cling to pleasure. Stay present and alert; don't lose yourself in heady analysis or emotional moodiness. Stay present and alert; God is fully present to you in each moment of your life, and prayerful alertness is the door into the awareness of God's presence.

**God, help me to stay
present and alert.**

The Present Moment

April 18

"Sloth is the great enemy."
Yoga Sutras

In my college years, I would meet with my spiritual director at least once a month. On one occasion, I showed up 20 minutes late. My spiritual director, a Franciscan nun, told me I was rude. When I protested that she was overreacting, she replied, "Time is a great gift; don't waste it! "Time is a canvas which allows us to paint images of creativity, love, compassion, and goodness. As such, time is a precious gift from God and should never be taken for granted. Laziness does nothing but waste time and is therefore a great tragedy. Don't waste time. Bring your will, your passion, and your soul to each moment, to every person, to all circumstances. Live purposefully, consciously, and intentionally. Prayerfully choose to be an instrument of God's peace to everyone, including yourself. If you live in this manner, your soul naturally becomes a brush in the hands of the Master Painter; your life, a masterpiece of Divine Art.

**God, if I am wasting the time
you have given me, show me.**

The Present Moment

April 19

"The awareness that everything comes from the same source filled Saint Francis with tremendous affection for all creatures."
Donald Spoto

Someone once asked the Dalai Lama if he was ever lonely. He emphatically answered, "No!" Most likely, the Dalai Lama never experiences loneliness for many reasons. Chief among them is the fact that he treats everyone he meets as a dear friend, be they presidents or peasants. If you want to experience God's presence moment by moment, be a friend to everyone you meet. Make eye contact. Say please and thank you. Bless everyone with your smile. If you are taking people for granted you are also taking God for granted; Jesus said so! If you are providing a service for someone, do it as if you are doing it for God – because you are. In the afterlife you will recognize God to the extent that you were willing to see God in the people around you in this life.

May I treat everyone else as a dear friend, including myself.

The Present Moment

April 20

"Therefore we shall receive all things with an equal soul from the hands of the Master."
Sri Aurobindo

It is easy to stay in the moment if the moment is pleasant. But what about moments of pain or misfortune? First of all, we must realize that it is not so much about staying in the moment as it is about staying consciously connected to God in all moments. Moments of distress are no exception, because God is in the distress too. Each instant of time is a sacrament containing the mystery of God's will. Our job is to remain in the center of our souls where no tempest can enter, saying to ourselves, "God is present in this pain. Instead of resisting or denying the pain, I will seek to be God's instrument within it."

**God, you are present
in each instant.**

Craig Bullock

The Present Moment

April 21

"If you do your best but still fail, give your failure to God. And make Him responsible for it."
Yogananda

Let us be honest. We are all going to have moments in which we fail, make mistakes, or fall short of our highest aspirations. When we have such a moment, our tendency is to flee out of guilt or shame. We must remember, though, that everything belongs to God, including our failures. As Yogananda said, give your failures to God and make them His responsibility. After all, God made you the way you are. Thus, the burden ultimately belongs to Him. Then, all we need to do is move on to the next moment, trying to make that moment as loving and productive as we can.

God, you will take my disappointments in myself off my shoulders.

Living Grace

Practicing God's Presence

April 22

"Creation is a ladder leading us to God."
Saint Bonaventure

I have experienced moments in my life when I just wanted to give up, not in a suicidal sense, but in the desire to settle for being half-alive, without any drive or ambition. Fortunately, the impulse toward happiness always overruled my lethargy. We human beings are driven to delight, goodness, beauty, and truth. Not coincidentally, God is all of these things. Therefore, practicing God's presence is not obsessing over the word "God" but willingness to enter into experiences of delight, goodness, beauty, and truth. Today, are you willing to bow before the beauty of a tree or a flower? Today, are you willing to embody goodness in your words and deeds? Today, are you willing to let truth guide you in all your affairs?

May I recognize you in all that is delight, goodness, beauty, and truth.

Craig Bullock

Practicing God's Presence

April 23

"Who are you, God, and who am I."
A prayerful mantra of Saint Francis of Assisi

Quite often, the biggest barrier to the awareness of God's presence is our false sense of self. We believe that we are separate, isolated personalities, cut off from God and others. Such a misperception automatically creates fear and anxiety. As an antidote to the false-self syndrome, I suggest that you try an experiment. As often as possible, refrain from using the pronouns "I," "me," or "my." These pronouns reinforce our identification with the personality and intensify our sense of separateness, thus deepening our suffering. In letting go of pronouns, we begin to experience a peaceful expansiveness, which is the beginning of the experience of God.

I am not my personality, my mind, my body, my past, or my problems.

Living Grace

Practicing God's Presence

April 24

"Love the Lord your God with all your heart."
Jesus

Spiritually minded people tend to view desire and passion as an evil to be avoided. Misdirected passion can cause great suffering and should be avoided. The purest form of passion, however, is the force of Divine Love moving us in the direction of truth, beauty, and goodness: toward God. Practicing the presence of God is the willingness to love the people in our lives fiercely, not feebly. God loves us fiercely! C.S. Lewis once said, "God is wild, you know." In the service of God we are called to be lovingly and passionately wild.

You love me fiercely!

Craig Bullock

Practicing God's Presence

April 25

"You must daily pick up your cross and follow me."
Jesus

Many on the spiritual path associate God, almost exclusively, with pleasant experiences. Many see adversity as something outside the realm of God and an evil to be avoided. We must resist such dualistic thinking. Paradoxically, adversity is the catalyst for a deeper and more expansive spiritual life. Adversity drives us into the depths of our souls where we discover levels of intelligence, intuition, strength, and grace that we didn't know we had. We should never look for adversity, but when it comes our way we should embrace it with prayer, faith, and hope. We should view adversity as a gift which God gives in order to divinize our consciousness and our lives.

**God, may I have the grace
to see adversity as gift.**

Practicing God's Presence

April 26

"Joy is the greatest defense against the snares of the devil."
Saint Francis of Assisi

Laughter is a great gift of God. Did you know that angels cannot laugh? Laughter requires a body, which angels do not have. Never underestimate the power of laughter. It cleanses our system of emotional and psychological debris and opens our hearts to God's grace. It is especially important to laugh at ourselves; taking ourselves too seriously blocks our awareness of God's presence. When we enjoy good-natured laughter, we practice God's presence. If you want to be a saint, learn to laugh deeply, fully, and often. Yogananda said, "A sad saint is, indeed, a sad saint."

God, save me from my seriousness and laugh in me.

Solitude

April 27

"Seclusion is the price of greatness."
Yogananda

Whether we call it karma, habit, or conditioning, our lives are driven by momentum. This momentum influences our thoughts, emotions, and actions, thus determining the quality of our lives. Solitude is a willingness to step outside the thrust of karmic momentum, a step which will give us a well-needed break from our habitual patterns. Solitude is neither an escape from life nor a flight into introversion. Simply, solitude gives God an opportunity to tweak our momentum – always in the direction of greater freedom, joy, truth, and love.

**You wait patiently for me to make time
and space for you alone.**

Solitude
April 28

"Contemplative silence is nothing else but a secret, peaceful, and loving infusion of God, which, if admitted, will set the soul on fire with the spirit of love."
Saint John of the Cross

Cell phones, computers, televisions, radios – we have an epidemic of noise in our culture. More than ever, we need solitude as part of the spiritual life. For most of us, solitude is a daunting endeavor because we all suffer, more or less, from an anxiety disorder. We are anxious about being good enough, about being alone, about having enough of what we need, about the future. Without our day-to-day distractions, our fears and phobias are bound to surface, so we tend to avoid solitude. The good news is that solitude does not mean that we are completely at the mercy of our inner negativity. Yes, our anxieties will surface and we will uncover more and more of our demons, but we will face them in the context of prayer, meditation, faith, the guru's grace and God's love. Their power over us will fade, and we will know God's sweet, simple, and profound presence.

I am never alone with my fears.

Solitude

April 29

"First keep peace within yourself; then you can also bring peace to others."
Thomas à Kempis

The noises of the external world tend to stimulate and reinforce the cravings of the false self, creating a type of egoic hunger pains. The ego resists prayerful solitude because the ego cannot exist in isolation; there is simply nothing to feed it. But if we persist, our solitude eventually gives birth to the true self, the divine image of God. As the true self rises within our awareness, we experience less and less loneliness, even when we are alone, because we are one with our souls and with God. The grand paradox is that the more comfortable we are with being alone and living from our souls, the more capable we are of being deeply connected to others.

God, may I learn to recognize my egoic hungers, let them go, and turn to you.

Solitude
April 30

"The kingdom of heaven is like a merchant in search of fine pearls, who, on finding one pearl of great value, went and sold all that he had and bought it."
Jesus

God offers more out of our willingness to wait on Him in solitude than we can imagine. In solitude, we will eventually discover what the mystics refer to as "spaciousness." Spaciousness is far from empty space. It is an infinite field of Divine Presence which encompasses everything and everyone. We experience this spaciousness as loving fullness, completeness, or bliss. As we open to spaciousness through prayerful solitude, we become larger, fuller, and more spacious internally. In yet another paradox of solitude, our horizons are not diminished but rather expanded. We become more compassionate and inclusive, more God-like. Making room in our lives for prayerful solitude is, therefore, an act of loving kindness toward God and ourselves.

Divine Beloved, help me to welcome times of solitude wherein I may welcome you.

The Guru

May 1

"The soul is the true and immortal nature of man. The nature of the soul is spirit: ever existing, ever conscious, ever-new joy."
Yogananda

Prior to my journey into Kriya Yoga, many of my spiritual endeavors were focused on healing or perfecting my personality – a frustratingly impossible task. Yogananda taught me a liberating truth: I am more than my personality, more than my psychological tendencies, and more than my self-image. I am a soul, fashioned in the very image of God. Our souls do not need saving; we just need to re-discover our true identity. We make that re-discovery in meditation. When we go into the silence, all of those interior voices that want to define and control us begin to weaken, and eventually they pass overhead like clouds. Only a simple but profound awareness, marked by peace and freedom, clarity and joy, remains. Yogananda never asked to be worshiped. Like all great saints and mystics, he is a perfect mirror who reflects our own divine possibilities.

Guruji, as I gaze upon you, let me see the divinity in myself.

The Guru

May 2

"I shall always be watching over each one of you."
Yogananda

In the modern world, we tend to have a very limited understanding of life. For example, we only believe what our five senses can perceive. Yet virtually all of the world's religious traditions testify to the existence of unseen worlds and astral realms which are intimately involved in our own experiences. Those great masters who have left their bodies, such as Jesus, dwell within these heavenly spheres. Their grace, wisdom, and love are freely available to us merely for the asking. As you move through your day, speak to Jesus, Yogananda, Francis, or the Blessed Mother as if they are your best friends, because that is what they are. Yogananda said, "Whenever a devotee thinks of me, in the depths of his soul, he will know that I am near."

My Beloved, My Teacher, My Friend

Craig Bullock

The Guru

May 3

"The guru is just as important as God, perhaps even more so, because without the guru we will never find God."
Gregorio Torello

If we had no need for a guru, we would all be enlightened saints and the world would be heaven on earth. Neither is true. Our minds are too distracted by cares and our intentions have been hijacked by our desires. The guru stands in our midst as a door into the Divine Life. Walking through the door begins with trusting that the gurus know far more than we do, and that they can indeed bring us home. Secondly, we must hope in the gurus, for their light is strong enough to literally lift us out of darkness. Lastly, we must love the gurus. Loving the gurus is not completely emotional; it is also the willingness to absorb ourselves in their teachings, their mission, and in their grace-filled presence.

**My guru, I need you. I trust you,
I hope in you, and I love you.**

Perpetually In God

May 4

"God is love."
The Apostle John

In a lifetime, many people imprint their words upon us. Some of these words are life-giving, and others are destructive. We must be very discerning about whose words we internalize. Of course, God's words are always true, perfect, and liberating. At the dawn of creation, God spoke a powerful, pristine Word. That Word held the seed of every human being that was to be born, including you. Each of us has existed in God's mind for all of eternity; God knew us before we knew ourselves. We are neither a cosmic roll of the dice nor an accident; we have been loved into existence by a God who is love. We are known, understood, and infinitely valued. Don't internalize the world's definition of you, and don't buy into a false spiritual view that says you are evil or just an insignificant cog in the play of creation. God has been having a love affair with you for all of eternity. Spirituality is simply the process of waking up to who we really are, and to the One who perfectly loves us just as we are.

**Beloved, help me to believe
that I am eternal.**

Perpetually In God

May 5

"Never call yourself a sinner. You are a child of God."
Yogananda

Yes, God has lovingly created all of us. We are all part and parcel of the one, Divine Life, fashioned in God's image. Yet, we are not carbon copies of one another. God has specifically endowed all of us with a sacred uniqueness, and each of us reflects God's splendor in an absolutely unique manner. We all matter. We all make a difference. We are all essential pieces in the God puzzle. Creation would be incomplete without you! Therefore, do not hang your self-esteem on what others say about you, and never define yourself according to your successes or failures. You are the apple of God's eye. Spirituality is, in part, learning to see yourself as God sees you, to experience yourself as God experiences you, to enjoy your life even as God enjoys your life!

**Without my soul living this life,
the puzzle of your creation is incomplete.**

Perpetually In God

May 6

"Seek and you shall find."
Jesus

Saints are not always mild-mannered in their approach to life and to God, and neither should we be. Some of my most profound spiritual experiences occurred when I dared to be real with God. The truth of the matter is that God spoke you into existence using the only language God knows: love. If you want God to hear your prayers you must speak God's language. Be honest, be sincere, be real, be raw; just speak from your heart. Flood heaven with your tears, and yell if you need to; whisper if it makes sense. Do not be nice, neat, and appropriate in God's presence. Be a wild, crazy lover. Don't you know? Saints are insane with love. Plead your case, confess your sins, or weep with gratitude; just speak from your heart – because your heart is, in reality, God's only ear.

May I be insanely in love with you.

Perpetually In God

May 7

"A saint is a sinner who never gave up."
Yogananda

Being human is a sloppy, unpredictable affair. We make mistakes. We say things we regret. We hurt the ones we love. We forget our promises. But we also manifest great heroism, creativity, and goodness. We forgive those who hurt us, we sacrifice our lives for others, and we never quite give up on love. Don't despise your imperfections! Why? They are the very portals by which God enters our hearts. Besides, nothing new or life-giving can unfold without a bit of sloppiness. God finds our humanity to be very, very endearing. So should we.

I am both your mess and your glory.

Perpetually In God

May 8

"In my image and likeness I created them; male and female I created them."
The Book of Genesis

What a wonderful gift it is to be born a human being! Not only are we embodied awareness and part and parcel of material creation, but we are capable of enjoying a good meal, a beautiful sunset, and the physical touch of a loved one. Did you know that angels are not blessed with the gift of laughter? You need both an evolved mind and a body to laugh. In addition to these physical blessings is a spiritual reality that we can hardly comprehend: our souls are the very Image of God. We can consciously commune with God and enter into the deepest states of bliss. Not only can we feel love; we can become love. We are, quite literally, the marriage of heaven and earth. What does this mean? Don't despise your humanness. Embrace it, celebrate it, and enjoy it. At the same time, don't deny your divinity. Pray from your deepest depths, dive into the Great Silence; be God's presence to everyone and everything. Thank God for the privilege of being you!

God, you and I live this life together.

Craig Bullock

Perpetually In God

May 9

"The Om vibration is the mother of all sounds; this holy vibration is the link between matter and God."
Yogananda

The Bob Dylan song Lay Down Your Weary Tune contains a line that recently caught my attention: "The ocean wild like an organ played." I wondered, who is playing the ocean like an organ? The answer is, of course, God. Literally, God is the unseen force perpetually "humming" creation into existence. Unlike all other species, we humans are actually capable of directly experiencing God's life sustaining hum, which is the Breath of God or the Holy Spirit. Yogananda stated that the mantra Om, when chanted with attentive devotion, links us to God's Spirit, saturates us with Divine Life, and empowers us to be a force for peace and healing. As you move through your day, inwardly chant Om until you feel its vibration in every fiber of your being. One of my favorite variations of this sacred mantra is, "Om God, Om Christ, Om Guru." Find the form that works best for you, and inwardly pray it with all of your heart and soul, giving God permission to make your life into a beautiful, sacred song!

Om God, Om Christ, Om Guru.

Perpetually In God

May 10

"How can I truly be in heaven when those I love are in hell?"
David Bentley Hart

We become most human, reaching our highest potential, not in great conquests, great wealth, or in great spiritual insights. No, we realize our highest destiny in loving God and others. Now, let's put some bite into this spiritual truth. Abraham Lincoln said of heaven, "It's everyone or no one." Yogananda stated that he would "come back again and again to bring lost brothers home to God." The truth is, we will not be able to enjoy the highest heaven if any of our loved ones are suffering in a personal hell. If we are truly God-realized, we will spend our eternity, our bliss, and our freedom liberating others. That is heaven; that is humanity at its highest apex. Amen!

**Divine Mother, you will bring
all of us home.**

Fearlessness

May 11

"There is no fear in love. Perfect love casts out all fear."
The Apostle John

Growing up in the inner city and having to be tough to survive, I learned to deny any semblance of fear. But denying fear does not make it go away. Denial simply pushes fear underground where it begins to do even more damage. What I have learned since I embraced the spiritual path is that the only antidote to fear is love. To know God is to love God — because God is perfect love. God's love is the momentum or force that opens our hearts, heals our wounds, and unites us as people. The enemy of love is not hate, but fear. Fear blocks us from experiencing love because it constricts the heart. If we wait for circumstances to be ideal in order to let go of our fears, we will remain mired in fear forever. Freedom from fear is the fruit of placing our attention entirely on God, no matter the circumstances. God has created us to live fearlessly and lovingly!

**God and guru, help me
to let go of all fear today.**

Fearlessness

May 12

"You are a child of God. What have you to fear?"
Yogananda

The entire human race suffers from an anxiety disorder: we all carry within us layer upon layer of fear, which is the primary source of human suffering. Fear constricts our minds, bodies, hearts, and spirits. To the extent that we are constricted, God's light is not free to penetrate into the depths of our consciousness. Sooner or later, we must confront our fears. The first and most important fear we must confront pertains to God. Despite our apparent sophistication, many of us still harbor within the depths of our psyches a primitive fear of God in the context of hell, judgment, abandonment, disapproval, rejection, or indifference. Forever watching our backs, we are afraid to trust God's goodness. The good news is that spirituality is the ever-deepening process of discovering God's inexhaustible generosity, wonder, and love.

Divine Mother, dissolve all my fears, especially any fears about you.

Fearlessness

May 13

"When worries howl at you, drown their noises, loudly chanting, God, Christ, Guru."
Yogananda

Two common, deeply rooted primal fears deal with economic insecurity and a sense of personal inadequacy. Most of us spend enormous amounts of energy doing our best to deny, repress, or avoid the anxieties associated with these fears, but sooner or later they will bubble up into our awareness. Such is the human condition. We will not resolve these fears in endless cycles of analysis or by trying to fix ourselves. When we learn to prayerfully place the eyes of our souls on God and to rest in God's goodness, protection, and love, we will find the real solution. This interior rest is an act of faith. Our faith does not mean that we will never experience anxiety, but it does mean that God's grace will keep us from being overshadowed by these primal fears – which is the beginning of true freedom.

God, Christ, Guru.

Fearlessness

May 14

"Fear not; it pleases the Father to give you the Kingdom."
Jesus

Believe it or not, fear is entirely unnatural; God has created us to live without it. Fear arises within human consciousness as a result of delusion. We fear because we believe we are separate from God, left to our own devices, and entirely responsible for ourselves. This false belief spawns anxiety and deep levels of inadequacy. Yet at every moment of the spiritual life, God is lovingly coaxing us out of fear.

Overcoming fear, though, has nothing to do with optimism, blind faith, or positive self-talk. The antidote to fear is truth! Truth is not primarily an intellectual argument, but an experience of reality. Our reality is that we "live and move and have our being in God," which means that we are always in the center of God's providence, purpose, and power. The more certain we become of this truth, the more our fears dissolve into nothingness.

**God and guru, instill Truth
deep within my being.**

Fearlessness

May 15

"Faith is a matter of an act of the free personality in the face of complete silence from heaven and earth."
Valentin Tomberg

Without faith in God's wisdom, goodness, and love, fearlessness is impossible. In today's world, however, faith is hard to come by. We tend to be cut off from nature and the spiritual world, both of which bring us into contact with God and help to inspire faith. Without this contact, we are mired in doubt. We rely only on what our senses or reason tells us rather than trusting the intuition of our souls. All pilgrims on the spiritual path are sooner or later confronted with the necessity of making a simple, pure act of faith, which neither God nor guru can do for us; we must make this act of faith ourselves. What is an act of faith? It is choosing to live our lives as if God is absolutely good, loving, and trustworthy – even when all of heaven seems silent. Such faith eventually leads to conscious contact with God, which begets fearlessness.

My God, I choose faith in you.

Fearlessness
May 16

"To be caught up in fear, anger, greed, or any violent or impulsive emotion is to forget God. If your senses, which govern your emotions, are under your control, you are a saint."
Yogananda

When I was a child, we were more or less told to "stuff" our feelings. These days, we are encouraged to express, indulge, and act on our every emotional whim. Both approaches are wrong! We have feelings, but we are always more than our feelings. Because we are the Image of God, our souls at the most essential level are depthless reservoirs of Divine Peace. If we are wise, we will learn to live from our souls so that we can deal with our emotions from a place of God-inspiration. Sometimes we will take our feelings seriously; at other times, we will merely witness them, always guided by the intuitive forces of truth, beauty, and goodness. The spiritually mature person directly influences his or her emotional life for the good by consistently attending to God's loving presence within, and by nurturing thoughts of peace, hope, joy, and fresh possibilities. Yogananda teaches us, "In God alone one finds ever new joy."

**Your love is always
the greatest part of me.**

Fearlessness

May 17

"We should train ourselves to think in grand terms: Eternity! Infinity!"
Yogananda

God is neither petty nor small minded. God not only sees the big picture, God is the big picture. Since we are part and parcel of God, we are also part and parcel of the big picture, playing our roles in the grand play of creation. Our bodies change, grow old, and eventually die, but we live forever in the flow of a grand and glorious plan. Why do we allow ourselves to get upset about so many things, from the size of our waistlines to the current state of politics? I am not suggesting that we abandon our responsibilities. Rather, I am challenging you not to lose your soul in the muck and mire of life. I am challenging you not to sweat the small stuff – and even death is small stuff. I am challenging you to keep the eye of your soul on the guru. The only way we make a real difference in the day-to-day happenings on planet Earth is to operate from the big picture, from God's loving, eternal perspective.

Eternity! Infinity!

Judge Not
May 18

"Whatever you do to the least of my brothers and sisters, you do unto me."
Jesus

Spiritual people live purposefully and alertly. As we daily interact with others, we are also influencing them through our words, body language, attitudes, and actions. A simple but powerful spiritual practice is consciously choosing to bring out the best in all the people we encounter. Withholding judgment is the beginning of this choice. The human spirit is rich, deep, complex, and far beyond our ability to comprehend. We may discern that another's behavior is unhealthy or destructive, as in the case of addiction, but we have no right to condemn another. God wants us to look for the inherent divinity of all people. With heartfelt sincerity, we can listen, smile, encourage, appreciate, and acknowledge. By appreciation of the best in others, we allow God to bring out the best in us. Spiritual progress is not measured by pleasant meditations, but by our capacity to love.

Beloved God, I need never judge another of your children.

Judge Not

May 19

"Do not judge."
Jesus

None of us has the right to judge and condemn others. Neither is it our responsibility to judge or condemn ourselves. Yet we must remember that judgment and acknowledging truth are two very different things. Judgment is an emotional reaction to reality, an attempt to control what we don't like, or an impulse to play God. Judgment leads us into toxic shame, which has no place in the spiritual life. With discrimination, we can distinguish between truth and falsehood, between that which brings us closer to God and that which causes suffering. Truth sets us free. God never judges because "to know all is to forgive all." God understands our fears, pain, and ignorance; God sees the burdens that we carry not only from childhood, but from countless lifetimes. Thus, God sends us saints, sages, and avatars, not to judge us, but to bring us home. Day after day, lifetime after lifetime, God waits with open arms for our return.

Beloved God, help me to understand the difference between truth and judgment.

Judge Not
May 20

"Be merciful, even as your heavenly father is merciful."
Jesus

Jesus embodied God's mercy, the good news that we have been forgiven for everything! God is forever at peace with each one of us. Can we dare to believe that God holds no grudges and has actually forgotten all of our past misdeeds? We human beings possess an odd psychological tendency: we hang onto our neurotic guilt and self-hatred. We have become so identified with our negative self-images that we are afraid to let go of them; we do not know who we are otherwise, so we cling to our harsh judgments. Can we dare to let go of our self-hatred and enter into the freedom of God's love? Can we dare to let ourselves off the hook and accept the fresh start that God offers us? Today, prayerfully consider the possibility that God has truly forgiven you for everything and give yourself permission to taste the freedom of God's compassionate mercy.

**Beloved, give me freedom from myself
so that I may be free for you.**

Holy Thinking

May 21

"Freedom: that is God's greatest gift to us."
Yogananda

One of God's greatest gifts is the capacity to say no. Without it we would be mere puppets at the mercy of instinct, karma, and whim. Because we have the ability to say no we can fight against disease, injustice, and all manner of evil. The willingness to say no is absolutely essential for psychological and spiritual health. Saying no to our interior voices of criticism allows us to rise above the destructive energy of self-hatred and to open up to the experience of God's love. There is a paradoxical aspect to the word no. By saying no to our lower selves and our egotistical desires, we are also saying yes to heavenly treasures. We cannot say yes to God if we are unwilling to say no to those things that are not of God. Be grateful for your capacity to say no because it also empowers you to say yes to all God wants to give you.

**Inspire me to use the freedom
you give me to say no.**

Holy Thinking
May 22

"Read a little, meditate more, and think of God always."
Yogananda

Many years ago a wise mentor told me, "Mind your mind, because you will become what your mind focuses on." The human mind is like the moon. Just as the moon has no light of its own, neither does the human mind. The mind always reflects what it is focusing on – and what we focus on grows, because there is profound power in human consciousness. If we orient our minds toward truth, beauty, and goodness, our minds will reflect these aspects of God, psychologically, emotionally, and spiritually. As a start, ignore negative or fearful thoughts and pay attention to what elevates and ennobles you. If the dark thoughts are too strong to resist, then pray until God's Light dominates your awareness. When in doubt, always surrender your thinking to God.

**Not my thoughts,
but your thoughts.**

Holy Thinking

May 23

"Lord, make me your instrument."
Saint Francis of Assisi

The mind is not evil; it is merely a thought producing machine. Separate from God's Light, the mind can only manufacture distorted images, thoughts, and emotions, which do nothing but create suffering. But when we make the mind a servant of God, it becomes an instrument of truth, beauty, and goodness. To make the mind a servant of God, we practice prayerful silence and we expose ourselves to a wider and greater consciousness: that of a God-realized teacher. Placing ourselves at his or her feet, we must become docile receptors of God's light and allow that light to use our minds as a means of expression. Only then do our minds become enlightened. Today, do not focus your attention on pursuing pleasant experiences. Purposefully and consistently direct your awareness to God and guru and watch what happens to your thinking.

Guruji, my mind belongs to you.

Holy Thinking

May 24

"You are not the body or the ego, but the immortal soul...the reflection of the Spirit. Souls are radiating rays of Spirit."
Yogananda

Children tend to be happier than most adults because they come into the world free of an established self-image. Over time children are given messages – often negative messages – about who and what they are and should be. When our self-image is comprised of these negative voices, we suffer. If we are honest with ourselves, we will acknowledge a resistance to letting go of these painful messages because they define us; they have even become a security blanket of sorts. Who would we be without our self-images, even the painful ones? At some point in the spiritual journey, God and guru will ask us to let go of our self-images because they are false. The truth is that we are God's Image. The preparation for letting go of our illusory self-images is not some form of self-perfection, but the willingness to surrender everything to God, to Love – especially our real or imagined imperfections.

Without my negative self-image, I am simply the soul – a spark of your Divine Love.

Holy Thinking

May 25

"In my image I created them, male and female I created them."
The Book of Genesis

After finding God, nothing is more important than discovering our own identity. Let us begin with who we are not. At the deepest level of our being we are not our body, our gender, our sexual orientation, our race or ethnicity, our political party, our diagnosis, a saint or a sinner, or the stories we carry around about ourselves. If we attempt to quiet all our labels and stories by endlessly analyzing them, we will become paralyzed in a hell of self-preoccupation. In the highest heaven, all of our stories will fade away. Who we are cannot be captured with words or concepts because we are God's very image. Just as we discover God in unadorned silence, we only realize who we are in silence. Today, when the stories and labels arise, let them come and freely go without giving them any focus or energy. Fall into God, into your truest and purest self.

Dear God, stop me when I am tempted to focus on my stories about myself and turn me back to you.

Holy Thinking
May 26

"Every thought you think sets up a particular subtle vibration. When you mentally utter the word "God" and keep on repeating that thought within, you set up a vibration that invokes the presence of God."
Yogananda

Occasionally people ask me if I believe in hell. They are often surprised when I say that I have visited hell many times in my life. Then I explain that we are in hell whenever we have lost contact with our own souls and with God. The human mind is like a mirror which reflects in thoughts and feelings what it focuses on. If we consistently expose our minds to strife, tension, and negativity, we pollute ourselves with toxicity which engenders misery, pessimism, and depression. If we want to be a happy, successful force for good, we must consistently choose thoughts, images, and concepts which are life-giving. When we direct life-giving thoughts toward God, they become powerful prayers which are filled with the momentum of Divine Energy and Grace. So we must not allow our minds to wander here and there unattended and vulnerable to dark forces. We must remain alert, positive, clear, focused, truthful, and loving in thought, word, and deed. Holiness is the simple process of making our minds accessible to the mind of God. We become what we focus on.

I will keep my eyes on you.

Craig Bullock

A Mystical Look at Hell

May 27

"The sun shines on a piece of charcoal and a diamond. But the diamond receives and reflects the sun's light, whereas the charcoal does not. Similarly, all people are exposed to the light of God, but not all receive and reflect that light. To do so, they must purify themselves by meditation and by following the Ten Commandments."
Yogananda

Some say that religion is for those afraid of going to hell, while spirituality is for those who have been to hell. Hell is a level of consciousness whereby we have lost conscious contact with our own souls, and therefore, God. Hell is a place of suffering imposed on us not by God, but by the hand of our own ignorance. If we are honest, we will readily admit that we all carry pieces of hell within our own hearts; we are all mired in some level of delusion. We are all in need of liberation. The good news is that every time we pray, meditate, or seek to be an instrument of God's love, we allow the Light of Christ to illumine our souls. This Divine Light will elevate us out of the stubborn pockets of fears, attachments, and distortions which spontaneously haunt us.

**Beloved, you will do for me
what I cannot do for myself.**

A Mystical Look at Hell
May 28

"Ignorance of God is hell, as it engenders all manner of evils and burns away wisdom."
Yogananda

In Dante's epic Inferno the lowest level of hell is not fire, but a lake of solid ice. Satan is frozen in the ice up to his waist, furiously flapping his wings but unable to escape. The metaphor of ice is powerful on many levels, and it reminds us that hell is the complete absence of the warmth and light of God's love. In hell, we are frozen within ourselves and powerless to free ourselves from this eternal despair. Satan could not escape from hell because he was not willing to look beyond himself, to God, for his freedom. The good news is that God's love is a consuming fire capable of dissolving the thickest, most frozen of human hearts. Freedom from hell is always a process of entering into an ever-deepening relationship with God, God's messengers, and our human brothers and sisters. Each time we pray, meditate, entreat the gurus, express compassion for the suffering, or serve the needs of another, God elevates us out of our isolated darkness into the warmth of His light and love.

**Even though I walk in the valley of darkness
I will fear no evil, for you are at my side.**

Craig Bullock

Purgatory: Purification

May 29

"Man comes here on earth for the sole purpose of learning to break the chords that bind his soul."
Yogananda

Those from the Catholic tradition may refer to the concept of purgatory when they think of heaven and hell. Like hell, purgatory is neither a place nor a punishment. Purgatory is a process of releasing the fears, attachments, habits, judgments, and agendas that keep us from experiencing the fullness of God's love. The process of purgatory can occur in this life, in the afterlife, or in future lives. In this life, a purgatory experience is painful but ultimately liberating. When we leave this life we carry our earthly tendencies with us, but our experience of purgatory differs in an important way: in the afterlife, the experience of Divine Light is much more intense, powerful, and direct, so that we are better able to clearly understand ourselves, our souls, and higher spiritual realities. If we are willing, the transformation of our consciousness can occur quickly. A time of purgatory is a gift, albeit a painful one. Let us remember that no one desires our freedom and peace more than God and guru.

Beloved, with you I will have the courage to break the chords that bind my soul.

Heaven

May 30

"It is heaven all the way to heaven and hell all the way to hell."
Saint Catherine of Genoa

The belief that the moment one dies he or she becomes instantly and entirely God-realized is naïve. I know of no spiritual path or enlightenment tradition that teaches such a concept. Heaven is not a place, but a state of consciousness. The pockets of resistance to God's love which we carry here on Earth do not magically disappear when we leave the body; we take them with us. In God's Divine Mercy, the process of purification, surrender, transformation, or conversion does not end in heaven, or the astral realm, but continues into full and complete union with God and creation. Thus, the message is clear: we can enter into heaven now, in and through our willingness to love God, our neighbors, and ourselves. Then we will be free to spend our eternity doing good on earth – which is the very definition of heaven.

Beloved God, help me to choose to live from my liberated and heavenly soul.

Heaven

May 31

"God said, 'Let there be lights in the firmament of the heavens.. and let them be lights in the firmament of the heavens so as to give light upon the earth."
The Book of Genesis

About such things as heaven, Saint Paul said that we "see in a mirror, dimly." Thus, we must always approach the subject of heaven with a degree of humility. The world's saints and avatars have given us inspiring glimpses into the heavenly realm. In the Lord's Prayer, Jesus says, "Thy will be done on earth as it is in heaven." Heaven – as opposed to the lower astral worlds – is a dimension wherein God's will reigns supremely. All of heaven's inhabitants are aligned and attuned to God's light. Heaven, though, is not cut off from us. Heaven's inhabitants are keenly aware of our situations, challenges, and struggles. They constantly send us emanations of light, which manifest as wisdom, grace, peace, strength, and compassion. Likewise, our prayers and love for them reach them as waves of light, bliss, and comfort to help them on their journeys. Each time we pray, meditate, or act from compassion, we solicit a corresponding blessing from above. Heaven's light surrounds us to guide, inspire, and enlighten.

**I am never separate from
my loved ones, heaven, or you.**

Perpetually in God

June 1

"God is more inward to me than my inmost depths."
Saint Augustine

Even though we are capable of knowing much about ourselves, such as our psychological and social histories, or our genetic and cultural conditioning, none of these factors describe our deepest, most essential selves. Why? Each one of us is a unique expression of the Divine Image. Just as God is a rich and unfathomable mystery, so are we. A mystery can never be analyzed, probed, or measured, but only experienced and loved. As unique, beloved mysteries, we must avoid the temptation to put God and ourselves into categorized boxes. Be aware of your personality traits, but don't allow anything or anyone to define you. Ignore the ego's tendency to label everything, which obscures your actual identity in God. Not knowing is the beginning of true knowledge. Therefore, approach God and your innermost self with silence, awe, and childlike wonder. Dare to trust the mystery of God and the mystery of yourself. This is true freedom!

I do not need to understand everything about God, myself, or others.

Perpetually in God

June 2

"The entire universe is God's cosmic motion picture. Mankind's suffering is due to too closely identifying with one's role rather than the movie director, God."
Yogananda

God is neither a bearded old man nor an entrancing goddess. God is not a being among beings, not even a supreme being. Rather, God is the Root of all Roots, the Sourceless Source of everything and everyone, the Ground of all Existence. We draw our very existence from God's Being-ness. God's underlying presence perpetually sustains everything and everyone. Therefore, we don't have to run here and there searching for God, and we are free to let go of our happiness projects. Why? Because our souls are forever tethered to God's soul; otherwise, we would cease to exist. Through prayer, meditation, and silence, we must learn to dive into the interior depths of our own hearts. What do we discover there? God's simple, blissful presence and the fulfillment of the one desire that is at the core of all other desires: union with God. While fulfilling all of your duties today, stay anchored in your own soul, in God, and see how effortless everything becomes.

Beloved, the movie of this little life will be perfect.

Perpetually in God

June 3

"If something is complicated, God is not in it."
Saint Francis of Assisi

While our external lives are often very complex, our internal lives can be exceedingly complex. But our souls are radically simple because they are a reflection of God, and God is the very essence of simplicity. God does not have conflictual thoughts, diverse feelings, or confused motivations. God is just God: eternally simple and unchanging. Therefore, the more we move away from the complexities of our own minds and identify with our souls, the more Godlike we become. If we have two coats and we encounter someone who has none, we give him our extra coat. When in doubt, we tell the truth. If someone asks for our forgiveness, we give it because God is the very essence of mercy. Instead of trying to squeeze happiness from people, places, and things, we cherish the simple joys of life: friendship, a hearty meal, and good natured laughter. We effortlessly become full of gratitude because we know all good gifts, no matter how ordinary, have been given to us by God. Finally, we become less obsessed with ourselves, especially the compulsion to fix ourselves.

God, teach me to keep all things simple.

Perpetually in God

June 4

"Not even a lowly sparrow falls to the ground without the Father's knowledge.. The very hairs on your head are numbered."
Jesus

Over the past twenty years or so, many people have developed a notion of God that is similar to the Star Wars concept of "the force." Some believe that God is vague, impersonal energy which can be manipulated according to our own desires. Nothing could be further from the truth! God is Consciousness. Everything that happens, pleasant or painful, unfolds within God's all seeing Consciousness. In simple terms, we always have God's full, loving attention. Even more fantastic is the realization that our individual consciousness is a participation in God's Universal Consciousness. Spirituality is, in part, the expansion of our individual consciousness into the very Consciousness of God. This is why prayerful, meditative silence within the discipline of a daily meditation practice is so essential to the spiritual life. Silence has the power to heal our fractured, divided minds and to expand our hearts so that we are able to see and feel as God sees and feels. This is what it means to be human.

May I see with your eyes, not mine.

Perpetually in God

June 5

"God is not merely a name. God is the life surging within us, the life by which we see, in love, one another."
Yogananda

Our existence is not the result of a cosmic roll of the dice. Rather, we exist because God has loved us individually into existence, and that same love sustains us moment by moment. God is a perpetual fountainhead of loving generosity. And we, who are fashioned in God's very image, are happiest and most alive when we are being generative. Is it not true that our hearts flourish when we dare to love, to give, and to create? The problem is that most of us have been wounded by people and circumstances, so we close our hearts in an effort to protect ourselves from further hurt. Then we seek happiness by grasping after people, power, and possessions. As an antidote to fear, I ask you to prayerfully ponder the following truths: God is love, and God's love is the most powerful force within creation. Therefore, it is entirely safe to gamble everything you have, including your very self, for love!

Beloved, you will gently open my heart where it is closed.

Intuition

June 6

"Beyond the semi-intuitive conscience is pure intuition, the soul's direct perception of truth...the infallible Divine Voice."
Sri Daya Mata

As we mature in the spiritual life, our intuitive capacities grow. Intuition is not about seeing auras, mind reading, or predicting the future. Intuition is about discerning God's will, sensing what is true and good, and differentiating light from darkness. For intuition to develop, two things must happen: prayerful meditation which leads to interior calm, and the willingness to surrender our personal preferences so that we are truly open to God's guidance. As we grow, we will be guided by a sense of peace, rightness, and well-being. Our lives will unfold more smoothly and more lovingly. When you must make a decision today, stop, breathe, and ask for guidance. Then, trust the still, small voice within you.

**God and guru, show me
what is true and good.**

Intuition

June 7

"Learn to distinguish when inner guidance is an authentic intuitive message or only imagination and emotionalism."
Sri Daya Mata

How do we determine if our intuition is actually God's guidance or only wishful thinking? We know that our intuition is guided by God's loving wisdom because our lives will manifest the fruits of the Spirit: peace, joy, love, strength, clarity, kindness, faithfulness, self-control, truthfulness, and goodness. We must also be willing to seek the counsel of wise spiritual mentors or guides when we are faced with significant decisions. Intuition is the humble willingness to allow ourselves to be influenced by loved ones, teachers, angels, saints, and even strangers who come from God and guru. Our lives are not our own. They are a communal affair, the marriage of heaven and earth.

**Beloved, place your wise ones
in my path.**

Karma

June 8

"Peace I leave with you; my peace I give you. I do not give to you as the world gives. Do not let your hearts be troubled and do not be afraid."
The Gospel of John

We all have karma. What is karma? Karma is a propensity to experience life in a certain way according to habitual patterns. It is a persistent momentum which is unique for each of us. Karma is strong, stubborn, and deeply embedded in the human psyche. But there is one place and time where karma is entirely absent: the Great Silence. We are never more free than when we are nestled in God's stillness. If we want to rise above our karmic conditioning, we must enter into prayerful, meditative silence – every day of our lives. In silence, we are free to hear God whisper a new story line for our lives. We are free to receive God's grace and free to begin anew. In the Great Silence God and guru are able to elevate us above and beyond our present circumstances. Only the grace that flows from silence has the capacity to trump karma.

Let me always remember that grace trumps karma.

Karma

June 9

"Everyone is drunk with some habits. That is the hypnosis of karma."
Yogananda

It is always best to keep things simple. Karma, the tendency to experience life in a certain way, is not payback or punishment. Our genetics, early childhood experiences, race, culture, gender, and country of origin are just a few of the influences on our karmic fortunes. It is absolutely necessary to move away from the notion of "good" or "bad" karma. The karma we have is the karma we are supposed to have. Karma always serves our highest growth. Karma is God's gift to us because it wakes us up with an invitation to further our spiritual evolution. What are we going to do with our karmic gifts? Are we going to squander the opportunities karma brings to us, or are we going to maximize the blessings hidden in its challenges? No one can answer these questions for us, not even God.

**Beloved, help me to see my karma,
my whole life, as only gift from you.**

Karma

June 10

"I am the light of the world. He who follows me shall not walk in darkness, but shall have the light of life."
Jesus

Even though the influence of karma is wide-ranging and powerful, we do not have to be its puppets. We are made in God's image, and God is not influenced by karma. At the very core of our being is a point of pure consciousness, light, and freedom which is untouched by karma, sin, ignorance, family dysfunction, or even genetics. When by God's grace and the guru's guidance we learn to live from our souls, we begin to rise above karma's gravitational pull. Our souls reflect God's light, and when that light shines forth from our interior depths, karma's dark tendencies must necessarily vanish. What do light and darkness have in common? Nothing! In the simple disciplines of meditation, Kriya Yoga, holding prayerful silence, and seeking attunement to our gurus, our freedom is born.

My soul is a point of pure consciousness, light and freedom.

Karma

June 11

"What you experience in meditation, bring into your activity."
Yogananda

Without daily meditation, it is impossible to rise above the tentacles of karma. Meditation takes us into our interior depths where we encounter both God and our truest, deepest self. Here, there are no patterns, habits, compulsions, stories, or karma. There is only peace, presence, and the potential for everything that is good and life-giving. Our goal, in part, is to maintain a degree of conscious contact with God and our own souls, especially when we are engaged in external endeavors. Then, our words and actions will not spring forth from karmic compulsion, but from the freedom of truth, beauty, and goodness. Of course, we will forget our conscious contact with God and fall prey to karmic reactivity from time to time. But we do not have to remain stuck in the muck and mire of karmic conditioning. All that it takes to free ourselves is a moment of silence, the loving repetition of the guru's name, a prayer for help, and the choice to surrender all things to God... even our karma.

God and guru, give me the grace to know when I am stuck and the wisdom to ask for your help.

Karma

June 12

"Be of good cheer, for I have overcome the world."
Jesus

Both Jesus and Babaji overcame the karma of death. Lahiri Mahasaya trumped karma by raising a man from the dead and re-introduced Kriya Yoga to the world. Francis and Teresa overcame the karma of ignorance, fear, and selfishness and reinvigorated the Catholic Church with the spirit of truth, beauty, and goodness. Yogananda's ministry continues to liberate souls from the clutches of karmic suffering. Simply, a guru or saint of the highest order is much more than a teacher of wisdom. They embody divine energy, light, and love. When they release their grace, karmic shackles must fall! Today, pray to Jesus, Babaji, the Blessed Mother, and Yogananda for help, strength, and guidance. Meditate on their images and words. Humbly, lovingly, sit at their feet. Surrender everything to them so that God's grace can elevate you above the tentacles of karma and give you the life you were meant to live: the life of a Child of God.

Oh, Blessed Holy Ones, you wait to teach me, save me, and love me.

Karma

June 13

"There is a world revolution going on. In the karmic firmament of America I see a beautiful sign: that no matter what the world goes through, she will be better off than most other countries."
Yogananda

We see manifestations of karma's dark influence all over the world: war, terrorism, division, prejudice, and suffering. Against such a backdrop, the temptation to yield to fear, anxiety, and worry is great. It is all too easy to doubt the power of God's goodness and love. To live in a perpetual state of doubt is painful, even torturous. Those of us on the spiritual path are called to rise above these fearful machinations. We must dive into our souls, where faith in God's loving designs flourishes. Our souls know that God's love is the most powerful force in creation; that history must ultimately bow before God's truth; that all things work together for good. Today, when panic surrounds you on all sides, make a radical act of faith from the depths of your soul: pray, go into the silence, meditate, pray, surrender, smile, serve, and love.

Beloved God, you hold our suffering and our beautiful world in your heart.

I Am a Soul

June 14

"So God created man in His own image, in the image of God He created them; male and female he created them."
The Book of Genesis

Most of us suffer from a case of mistaken identity, identifying only with our fabricated self-images and personalities. The more we identify with this illusory "I," the more we suffer, and the more we cause others to suffer. But underneath the personality is the soul, our very own spark of Divinity. Simply, we do not have a soul; we are a soul. Inspired by God's love and wisdom, the soul constantly tries to break into our awareness to move us toward truth, beauty, and love. Spiritual maturity is learning to ignore the compulsive, controlling impulses that shoot forth from the personality; yet ignoring the personality is not enough. We must simultaneously attend to those inspired promptings of the soul which carry the scent of peace, hope, authenticity, light, strength, clarity, and compassion. Today, stay awake. Carry a degree of silence within so that you can hear God speak to you, in and through your soul.

I am a soul;
I am a part of you.

I Am a Soul
June 15

"God does not want us to think much, but to love much."
Saint Teresa of Avila

For most people, soul contact occurs more easily in and through the heart, but not the sentimental or romantic heart. Our physical and emotional awareness literally opens to the soul at the point behind our hearts. We make contact with our souls by placing our attention there whether we are breathing, thinking, speaking, or praying. When we experience self-forgetfulness, compassion, generosity, expansiveness, lightness, strength, calmness, and sincerity, we are in the flow of spiritual power which emanates from the heart. Eventually, the heart swallows the mind, bringing about a full and enlightened silence. Today, make a purposeful choice to stay connected to the point behind your heart. Let every word, action, thought, breath, and prayer come from your heart-center. Feel the grace and be happy!

**Beloved, with your grace,
may my heart swallow my mind.**

I Am a Soul

June 16

"Not my will, but Thy will be done."
Jesus

When we are imprisoned within our own distorted thoughts, assumptions, and feelings, we are living from the non-relationship of the false self. In contrast, our souls are open and always touching the very soul of God. Without our souls, we would cease to exist! We become conscious of our soul connection to the extent that our minds and hearts are turned toward God. No matter how lost we are in delusion and darkness, our soul's spark of freedom is never extinguished. We are always free to love and free to begin the journey back to God and our own souls. Every act of love toward God, every prayer, every meditation, every mantra, every heart-felt sigh, and every act of surrender gives God permission to draw us deeper and deeper into our souls and God's soul. When we live from the depths of our souls in conscious contact with God, we become our true selves.

God, give me a glimpse of how my true self, my soul self, would feel different from the self I think I am.

I Am a Soul
June 17

"Made a decision to turn our will and our lives over to the care of God as we understood Him."
The Twelve Steps

The false, egoic self – limited, fragmented, and overwhelmed – was never meant to manage life's challenges with any degree of peace. The false self cannot help but feel fragile. No amount of psychotherapy, analysis, or positive self-talk can save the false self from its inherent sense of inadequacy. Always remember that the consciousness that created our problems cannot solve them! A higher consciousness is needed. The good news is that our souls are already attuned to God's consciousness. Our souls are natural conduits to God's providence, guidance, and strength. Today, pray that you may avail yourself to the wisdom, peace, and grace that already exist within your soul. Surrender, so that God can take you beyond your limitations!

**Beloved, may I truly know
the meaning of Saint Paul's words:
"My grace is sufficient for you, for my strength
is made perfect in weakness."**

I Am a Soul

June 18

"The world's scriptures declare man to be not a corruptible body, but a living soul."
Yogananda

The self, the soul, is untouched by karma, conditioning, compulsion, sin, ignorance, addiction, genetic programming, and childhood trauma. Blissful and free, the soul effortlessly reflects God's light. Though we are naturally attracted to the soul, we also resist shedding the chains of the false self. We are so identified with the false self of the ego and the personality that we believe we are it and it is us. We want to save, perfect, and fulfill the false self. Letting go of the false self feels like a death of sorts, and it is. Even when we are motivated to shed it, its grip on us is formidable, like a gravitational field which keeps our awareness mired in the orbit of fear and delusion. Here, the grace of the guru is most important. When I gaze upon an image of Yogananda, I am pulled into my soul. When I receive Holy Communion, I am lifted out of my egoic self. When I read the words of Francis, I am immersed in soulful light. When I practice Kriya Yoga, my humanness becomes an instrument in the hands of God. When I sincerely surrender all things to God, my soul's peace fills me.

Above all else, I am a living soul.

I Am a Soul

June 19

"Blessed are the pure in spirit, for they shall see God."
Jesus

If we desire to be happy, free, and overflowing with love, we should repeatedly ask ourselves a defining question: Am I listening to my ego or to my soul? Our souls constantly release arrows of wisdom, guidance, and grace in the direction of our conscious minds. In order to receive them, we must want them more than we want our own habitual patterns. Sometimes we may think, "I shouldn't be so serious all the time." That thought makes it all too easy to fall back into a vegetative state and give in to our lower impulses. We then stumble, suffer, and become very critical of ourselves, which is never helpful. The goal is not to be morbidly serious, but to remain joyfully and calmly awake, in touch with our souls, and in loving communion with God and guru.

Beloved, to whom am I listening?

Karma Yoga

June 20

"Karma Yoga is the path of uniting the soul to God through selfless service."
Yogananda

Whether we are spending our time and energy pursuing money, fame, romance, security, power, or pleasure, we are all serving something. We would be wise to choose our pursuits carefully and prayerfully, because we become what we serve, what we love, and what we treasure. When we serve a cause, a person, or a path, we take on its inherent energy. Over time that energy shapes our thoughts, our feelings, and our consciousness. To the extent that we serve God, our lives become divine, luminous, and joyful. We do not have to run off to monasteries to serve God. Choose to selflessly serve everyone you encounter today and notice what happens to them and to you. God will happen!

**Grant me the joy
of selflessly serving you.**

Karma Yoga

June 21

"The spiritual man knows that duties to parents, children, family ties, the business world, and all else are to be carried out as service to God."
Yogananda

We become those things, people, and causes that we serve. If we want to be truly happy, we will seek to serve God in all areas of our lives, because God is the very essence of happiness. We should never complicate our understanding of service. It is very simple: stay alert at all times, be fully present to everyone you meet, choose to be joyful, let your words be filled with only truth and compassion, and pray to be an instrument of God's love in all circumstances. Though it is simple, it is not always easy. Be comforted that God is with you, providing you with all the grace you will ever need to live a life of service and happiness.

**Beloved, may I be fully present
to everyone I meet today.**

Karma Yoga

June 22

"Whatever you do to the least of my brothers and sisters, you do to me."
Jesus

Was Jesus kidding? Of course not! Jesus saw the world and its people through a non-dualistic lens; he experienced all of life as interdependent, connected, and unified. Jesus' heart was, and is, so big that he felt the joy and pain in the hearts of others, and everyone was his brother and sister. The pain of others moved him to compassionate action. Let us never forget that God resides in our husbands, wives, children, friends, neighbors, and enemies. We must learn to find God in others and also in ourselves. Our neighbors are an extension of us, we are an extension of them, and we are all an extension of God. When we bless a sad person with our smile, warmth, or concern, we are blessing God. It is that simple.

Move me to compassionate action.

Karma Yoga

June 23

"God does not want us to do great things, but small and simple things with great love."
Mother Teresa

For whom or what do we fulfill our duties? For ourselves? For material objects? For the reward of heaven after this life? If these things are our motivation, we are not free; we are slaves! God wants us to live as free men and women with grace and dignity. To live in this way we must learn to work only for God and for the alleviation of suffering in our fellow human beings. Yet working for God does not mean that we have to seek to do great things. Great men and women do ordinary things with great selflessness. God has given us plenty of people to serve. We just have to serve without attachment to outcomes, payoffs, or rewards. In all that we do, serve, and love, we are only working for the fulfillment of God's will. What comes of our efforts is God's business alone, and none of our business. This is true freedom!

I release my expectations of results, outcomes, and rewards to you.

Craig Bullock

Twelve Steps to Freedom

June 24

"We admitted we were powerless over our addiction, and that our lives had become unmanageable."
Step One

We spend so much of our energy trying desperately to impress others and ourselves – propping up our self-images, denying our pain, and feeling shame for our powerlessness. We are afraid of being seen as we really are. Thus, we hide from God, others, and ourselves, which does nothing but deepen our suffering. Part of the power of Twelve Step spirituality is that it is perfectly acceptable to be imperfect. We are free to drop our pretenses and finally come clean. Once we embrace it, powerlessness is the window through which God enters our lives and begins to lead us to freedom.

**God, grant me the serenity
to accept what I cannot change.**

Living Grace

Twelve Steps to Freedom

June 25

"Came to believe that a power greater than ourselves could restore us to sanity."
Step Two

We are all in over our heads, fighting wars we cannot win and struggling to avoid the quicksand of despair. Blaming others or ourselves only serves to mire us in more and more powerlessness. However, there is a heavenly power, grace, and energy available to all of us which is capable of moving us from the folly of self-sufficiency to hope. Hope is not wishful thinking, but the very light of God entering into our despair. Hope frees us to face our powerlessness and our addictions and offers us the promise of freedom, sanity, and a resurrected life. When we are in over our heads, we have only to look above, to God and guru.

Beloved God, you can restore me to sanity.

Twelve Steps to Freedom

June 26

"Made a decision to turn our will and our lives over to the care of God as we understood Him."
Step Three

When our suffering reaches a certain level of intensity and we have exhausted all our cleverness, we finally do what needs to be done. We look beyond ourselves, to God. We let go of the grip we have on our misery and allow God to take hold of us, surrendering our life and our will over to the care of God. We still feel the pull of our own desires, but we continually make the decision to trust God's wisdom over and against our own. We have learned that God is in charge of the world and we are not, and that God knows best. The fruit of surrender is sanity, freedom, peace, interior stillness, self-respect, and compassion for those who suffer. The ultimate fruit of surrender is the direct and immediate experience of God – otherwise known as God-realization.

You care for me. Help me to understand all that your care means in my life.

Living Grace

Twelve Steps to Freedom

June 27

"Made a searching and fearless moral inventory of ourselves... Admitted to God, to ourselves, and to another human being the exact nature of our wrongs."
Step Four and Five

God can only heal us to the extent that we let Him into the nooks and crannies of our souls. If we hide our darkness from ourselves and God, we run the risk of being blindsided by our shadow selves, causing unnecessary suffering. Ultimate freedom is standing naked before God so that God can lovingly take possession of us. Then we must stand naked before another person. If we cannot let another human being see us as we really are – the good and the bad – then we cannot really stand naked before God. What is true below is true above. To keep it real with God, we must be real with at least one other human being. Our realness is frightening, but ultimately liberating.

When you come to me in the guise of a trusted friend, help me to be real.

Twelve Steps to Freedom

June 28

"Were entirely ready to have God remove all these defects of character...Humbly asked Him to remove our shortcomings."
Step Six and Seven

Having character defects is part and parcel of being human. God understands. Yet, if we deny or indulge our character defects, they cause great suffering to ourselves and others. Most often, a character defect develops as a defense against pain, fear, or anxiety. Thus, we can only dare to let go of a character defect to the degree that we feel safe, secure, and loved. Twelve Step programs work because they situate people in the flow of spiritual energy, the energy of God's love. Love frees us to recognize our character defects and to seek God's help in letting go of them. We never save, enlighten, or liberate ourselves; only a higher power can do that. All that is ever required of us is a simple, persistent, and humble willingness, offered to God again and again. God does the rest!

**I will wait in quiet willingness
for you to remove my shortcomings.**

Twelve Steps to Freedom

June 29

"Made a list of all persons we had harmed and became willing to make amends to them all...Made direct amends to such people wherever possible except when to do so would injure them or others."
Step Eight and Nine

As we evolve spiritually, we feel a normal and healthy impulse to make amends for the pain we have caused. Making amends re-establishes balance in the natural order and allows grace to flow anew, bringing healing to both the offended and the offender. However, prayerful wisdom must prevail if an overt attempt to make amends can multiply the suffering of everyone involved. When this is the case, we must choose a different path. We may lovingly and persistently pray for someone we have harmed. We may quietly resolve to never again engage in hurtful behaviors. We may choose to make a donation to a charitable organization instead of directly refunding money to an individual. With the wisdom of our trusted friends and the guidance of our Higher Power, we will find ways to serve justice.

**God, grant me the courage
to change the things I can.**

Twelve Steps to Freedom

June 30

"Continued to take personal inventory, and when we were wrong promptly admitted it."
Step Ten

All of the world's spiritual traditions recommend a certain level of watchfulness over our thinking, feeling, and behavior. Watchfulness has nothing to do with obsessing, judging, or analyzing. Rather, it is the willingness to live consciously, paying attention to whether or not our thoughts, words, and deeds are in alignment with the momentum of truth, beauty, and love. Regularly taking a personal inventory is a way of being accountable to ourselves and God. Rather than inducing guilt or shame, such a practice allows us to live wisely, creatively, and with dignity. Admitting when we are wrong puts us at God's disposal and empowers us on the path to freedom.

Beloved, with your help I can see the truth and readily admit my mistakes without fear.

Living Grace

Twelve Steps to Freedom

July 1

"Sought through prayer and meditation to improve our conscious contact with God as we understood Him, praying only for knowledge of His will for us and the power to carry it out."
Step Eleven

If we are going to recover from our addictions – especially the addiction to our own thinking – we must establish conscious contact with God. We know that we are in conscious contact because we are not asking God to validate our likes and dislikes, but because we are willing to align ourselves to God's will, knowing that God always serves our highest good. However, praying for God's will is not enough; we must also pray for the power to carry God's will out. In praying for this power, we are telling God that we really mean business: we sincerely want to live our lives in alignment with God's purposes. Such heartfelt prayer draws the powerful forces of heaven to us, empowering us to live a Divine Life.

Thy will be done.

Craig Bullock

Twelve Steps to Freedom

July 2

"Having had a spiritual awakening as the result of these steps, we tried to carry this message to others, and to practice these principles in all our affairs."
Step Twelve

Spiritual transformation is not a haphazard affair. Such a process unfolds according to subtle, divinely established principles which are perfectly embodied within the Twelve Steps. The fruit of living these spiritual principles is a very real transcendental awakening whereby God becomes the organizing power within our lives, and our spirits become ever more sensitive to the movements of grace. The ultimate expression of such a transformation is an increased capacity to live our lives in the service of others and the healthy integration of spiritual principles into our daily lives. God increasingly lives and breathes in us, through us, and as us – the ultimate gift of sound, sober living.

**Beloved, may I freely give away
the gifts you have given me.**

The Garden
July 3

"The Kingdom of God is as if a man should scatter seed upon the ground, and should sleep and rise night after day, and the seed should sprout and grow, but he knows not how."
Jesus

The Book of Genesis shows us the setting which allows us to blossom psychologically, emotionally, and spiritually: a simple garden. A garden's prosperity is the work of man and God, the natural and the supernatural, human and divine will, man's effort and God's grace. Our mission is to cultivate our capacity for truth, beauty, and goodness, and to allow ripening and fruitfulness to unfold by God's spirit and in due season. A garden is a place of peaceful equilibrium which requires work, rest, grit, surrender, knowledge, and silence to operate together in perfect harmony. Today, tend your inner garden with loving care. Pray, cultivate silence, and plant seeds of loving kindness. In due time, the Divine Gardener will uproot the weeds of drama, impatience, and fear.

**You are the gardener;
I am your garden.**

The Garden

July 4

"To grow or to build? This is the choice that it comes down to in the last analysis."
Valentin Tomberg

Our lives are meant to be lived in a lush garden which is the fruit of our cooperation with God and God's cooperation with us. When we try to go it alone without the help of God or guru, we inevitably substitute a tower for a garden. The Book of Genesis tells us the story of the Tower of Babel, built by man in a misguided attempt at conquering heaven. The outcome of the tower building was only division and frustration. The towers that we build are our happiness projects, subjective assumptions, stubborn attachments, and illusory beliefs. A garden and a tower cannot exist within the same space. Nurturing a garden is really very simple: meditative silence, humility, prayer, love, compassion, faithfulness to truth, and obedience to the guru. It is the gentle growth of the Divine Life within and among us that we seek, not the construction of a spiritual, psychological, or ideological structure.

God, show me if I am building a tower instead of nurturing a garden.

The Garden
July 5

"Meditation with love and devotion cannot fail, in the long run, to bring you bliss everlasting and final union with God who is love."
Yogananda

We must do our part in cultivating our soul's garden through prayer, meditation, study, and service. Then we must wait and wait some more. No matter how hard we try, we cannot make seeds grow into plants or yield fruit according to our timetable. The timing is entirely up to the Divine Mother. Likewise, we cannot will ourselves into union with God. We must learn to wait in silence. But do not think that waiting is a waste of time. What happens in the waiting? All of our anxiety, impatience, grasping, willfulness, and resistance sprout into our awareness, causing considerable discomfort. Slowly but surely God removes these unwanted weeds, and the day comes when we find ourselves in a simple, sublime state of Divine Union. We don't quite know how it happened because it is a gift, a grace. We cultivate the garden, but only God can make it grow.

**Beloved, be with me
in the waiting.**

Holy Simplicity

July 6

"Seek first the kingdom of God, and everything else you need will be given to you."
Jesus

A truly simple life requires that we have one singular, underlying purpose that guides our lives and directs our thoughts, emotions, and decisions. If we are wise, we will make our love for God this singular purpose. This does not mean that we have to shun the world or shirk our responsibilities. It does mean that we do everything, even the most humble of tasks, as an expression of our love for God. When God becomes the love of our lives, all our human faculties become unified, and we become clearly focused in all that we do. Divine energy and inspiration energize us. Today, give your life to God. Pray to be nothing more than an instrument of heavenly wisdom, grace, and love. Watch and see how simple, peaceful, and powerful your life becomes.

**My love for you
is my singular purpose.**

Holy Simplicity

July 7

"Live simply... If something is complicated, God is not in it."
Saint Francis of Assisi

The spiritual life is always, always a simple life. Yogananda says, "Those who have attained God's kingdom are children in their simplicity and pure minds...they are non-attached, truthful, and trusting like a child." The ego complicates, confounds, and confuses everything, but the Holy Spirit simplifies everything. So choose to live simply! Pray and meditate every day, and surrender everything to God. Remember to laugh, and don't be afraid to cry. Do all things to the best of your ability. Share your abundance with others. Tell the truth. Do what is good, and avoid what is bad. Say please and thank you. Carry your wounds with grace and dignity. Don't be afraid to say "I'm sorry," and always forgive others. Give yourself permission to say "no." Smile at people. Seek to be an instrument of God's peace. Resist nothing and accept everything. Work, play, and take naps. Finally, show God a good time!

**Beloved, help me to be
content with simplicity.**

Holy Simplicity

July 8

"God is simple; everything else is complex."
Yogananda

Simplicity is being simple. Simplicity means that we fulfill our day-to-day duties with single-mindedness, completely present to the task at hand and to the people in front of us. Simplicity requires a level of self-forgetfulness. Instead of worrying about ourselves, our success, or our self-image, we choose to be absorbed in whatever we are doing at the moment. In this way, we become the work instead of someone who is performing the work or worrying about the work. The work itself has our complete focus. God can manifest mightily in and through such concentrated simplicity. Today, give your full attention to whatever you are doing in each moment, including having fun. Do it all for God. Forget yourself and be happy.

**God, grant me single-mindedness
and single-heartedness.**

Holy Simplicity

July 9

"God is simple...without diversity, defect, or interruption."
Saint Bonaventure

God is simple. God is love. God only loves, at all times and in all places. Clearly, the more evolved we become the more God-like we become, and the more simple we become. When our desires become simple, everything we do is motivated by love. Our sense of self is simple: we are God's children, made in God's image, and others are simply our brothers and sisters. Yet do not confuse simplicity with weakness. The simpler we become, the more effective, influential, and powerful we become. When our energy, intelligence, and will is focused and concentrated, all of our God-given powers are magnified. Steve Jobs, a devotee of Yogananda, said, "Simple can be harder than complex. You have to work hard to get your thinking clean, to make it simple. But it's worth it in the end because once you get there, you can move mountains."

**God and guru, give me the courage
to seek simplicity in a world
that prizes complexity.**

The Present Moment

July 10

"If I did not simply live from one moment to the next, it would be impossible for me to keep my patience. I can only see the present...It is such folly to pass one's time fretting, instead of resting quietly on the heart of Jesus."
Saint Therese of Lisieux

To the logically oriented mind, abandonment to Divine Providence makes no sense. But we do have the capacity to grasp the mysteries of God intuitively. One of those mysteries is the truth that God is present to us in the duties and opportunities of the present moment. We must stop our squirming and resisting what is and accept the present moment, be it pleasurable or painful, as a gift from God. Our job is not to ask "Why?" but to exhale and say to God, "As you wish." Today, ask for the grace to see your spouse, children, co-workers, humdrum responsibilities, challenges, and even yourself as God's gifts to you. Embrace, love, and celebrate them, because God gives us only what serves our growth and liberation. God can only love.

Beloved, as you wish.

The Present Moment
July 11

"Which of you by being anxious can add a cubit to the span of his life? Thus I tell you, do not be anxious about your life."
Jesus

If meditation centers us in God, then living prayerfully in the moment keeps us consciously grounded in God. The past is only good for recalling positive, loving experiences, and if we make wise, loving choices in the present, the future will absolutely take care of itself. Being fully present to God in the moment means that we concentrate on pulling ourselves out of the past and future. Quite literally, each and every moment is a sacrament overflowing with heavenly riches. When we find ourselves stuck in the past or lost in the future, we need to do only one thing: speak to God clearly, sincerely, and lovingly, while also looking God straight in the eye. Assuredly, God's grace will pull us back to the present moment – which is God's only abode.

Beloved God, bring me back to now when I am lost in the past and the future.

The Present Moment

July 12

"The manifest power of concentration comes from centering the mind on one thing."
Yogananda

God is always sending us love, guidance, inspiration, strength, courage, wisdom, and grace of all kinds. But many of us are not consciously aware of the Divine Energy flowing in our direction, not because we are unworthy, but because we lack the concentration. Far too often our awareness is scattered amid competing concerns, attachments, and desires. The art of concentration is not the same as being rigidly focused on something, and it is certainly not obsession either. Concentration begins with the willingness to organize our lives according to a centralizing energy or momentum. The more we concentrate our awareness on God's truth, beauty, and love, the more we are pulled into the gravitational field of God's presence, and the more our lives become a manifestation of the Divine Life, which is the experience of heaven, right here and right now.

Order my steps in your grace and energy.

The Present Moment
July 13

"The activity of God is everywhere and always present."
Jean-Pierre de Caussade

Let us get one thing straight: responsibility for the world belongs to God, not us. Nothing scatters the sense of God's presence more than worry, and worry occurs because we assume responsibility for things that are beyond the scope of our ability to manage. God gives us only one charge: to live the present moment peacefully, lovingly, and wisely – end of discussion. For example, God has not given any of us the assignment of creating world peace, but if we meet each moment with joy, compassion, and prayer, we will effortlessly contribute to the momentum of peace. Spiritual concentration is letting go of what is not our business. Our only business is the present moment and the responsibilities therein, to be lived for the love of God.

Divine Mother, teach me to let go of what is none of my business.

Meditation

July 14

"Jesus breathed on his disciples and said, "Receive the Holy Spirit."
The Gospel of John

There is only one essential ingredient to a meditation practice: love. We don't meditate to have pleasant experiences. Rather, we meditate because we love God and desire to experience loving union with God. Breath provides the path. Unlike physical breathing, spiritual breathing requires our conscious participation. With our conscious, spiritual breathing we breathe in God's Breath, God's Spirit, and God's Presence. When we breathe in God's Spirit we are actually inhaling Divine Love! As you move through your day, breathe with awareness. As you consciously breathe, remember God, and speak God's name with sincerity and love. Let your breath become a living prayer.

My breath is your breath.

Meditation
July 15

"Any devotee practicing the science of meditation can satisfy the thirst of mortal desire by renouncing inner desires and reversing the outwardly flowing currents of consciousness and life energy and uniting those currents with the ever new bliss of God."
Yogananda

Many of us have a misconception about meditation: that meditation will facilitate the manifestation of our desires. But meditation actually accomplishes the opposite: it brings our noisy cravings to a standstill. Many of us resist the discipline of meditation because we know that it is the beginning of the end of our ego-driven desires. Whether we believe it or not, a river of grace and love exists within all of us. Can we dare to take Jesus, Yogananda, and the world's mystics at their word?

If you cannot, try meditation as a scientific experiment. Meditate thirty minutes a day for thirty days. Never judge a meditation by how pleasant it might or might not be; meditation always works. Know that during each sincere meditation God will flood your soul with light and divine energy. Day by day your attachments to unhealthy habits will diminish, and you will experience a growing sense of peace.

**A river of grace and love
flows within me.**

Meditation

July 16

"Silence is the sign of real contact with the spiritual world, and this contact, in turn always engenders the influx of heavenly forces."
Valentin Tomberg

God needs a consistent level of meditative silence from us because prayerful silence quiets our desires and willfulness. When our willful desires are quieted, we are no longer infatuated with lesser gods, and God's Spirit easily moves in and through us, making us instruments of His love and wisdom. Silence not only allows us to rest in God but also engenders real contact with the heavenly realms, allowing saints, gurus, and angels to accompany us in the fulfillment of our missions. At first we may only be able to experience silence for a moment. Then, single moments become many moments. Eventually, we become prayerful, hushed temples of God's love.

**Gurus, angels, and saints,
be with me.**

Suffering
July 17

"The truth is that life involves suffering."
Buddha

Though my childhood years were less than perfect, they were stable, safe, and relatively serene until my mother died when I was twelve years old. Quite naturally, her death shook my world to the core. For the first time I experienced real suffering. Yet in a mysterious way, this time of suffering was also the beginning of my spiritual journey. Suffering is never a punishment – it is against God's nature to punish. Suffering does crack the shell of our illusions, denial, and smugness while also opening us to the experience of God's loving, healing presence. I am not glorifying suffering, but I am saying that suffering is often the necessary door to freedom, enlightenment, and God. Since life is not a roll of the cosmic dice, the suffering that comes to us is the exact suffering we need in order to grow, evolve, and wake up to God's wondrous presence.

**My precise suffering
is never an accident.**

Suffering

July 18

"Humbleness is the open gate through which the divine flood of mercy and power flows into receptive souls."
Yogananda

A big part of the reason we suffer is that we are infatuated with our minds – actually addicted to our own thinking. We must be willing to let go of our thoughts about everything, including God and ourselves. The problem with letting go of our thoughts is that they are a security blanket of sorts which gives us the illusion of control and safety. Additionally, most of the thoughts we think are nothing more than recycled concepts with little fresh insight, creativity, or value. Years ago, a saintly man told me, "I have always felt God's love and protection all around me, so letting go has been easy." The truth is that we are all loved by God, equally! We are all protected by God, equally! We are all guided by God, equally! Thus, we can let go of our hardened, limited, and distorted thoughts about God and ourselves because God will always catch us.

Beloved, help me to be humbly realistic about my mind's abilities.

Suffering
July 19

"If we believe, then everything is illuminated and takes shape around us: chance is seen to be order, success assumes an incorruptible plentitude, and suffering becomes a visit and caress of God."
Teilhard de Chardin

Either God is everywhere, or God is nowhere; we cannot have it both ways. The world's mystics proclaim the truth that God is embedded in everything and everyone, working to bring about the healing of all creation. God is embedded even in our suffering, working from the inside out to transform our minds and hearts. To the external eye, nothing but the decay of Jesus' body was happening as he lay in a cold, dark tomb. But underneath it all, God was transforming his body into a living, breathing manifestation of light and love. We should neither glorify nor indulge our suffering, but we should bear it with childlike trust in this certainty: God, hidden in our suffering, is working to liberate us so that we too can be manifestations of divine light and love.

Beloved, you are hidden deep within my suffering, forever working to liberate me.

Craig Bullock

I Am a Child of God

July 20

"Truly, I say to you, unless you become like a child, you will never enter the kingdom of heaven."
Jesus

One Christmas, a disciple of Yogananda's gave him a squirt gun as a present. Saying nothing, Yogananda tucked the gift within the fold of his swami's robe. For weeks afterwards he gleefully went about squirting many of his followers. Though a great saint, Yogananda clearly possessed many childlike qualities. Children come into the world much more connected to God. The fruit of this connectedness is evident in the fact that they laugh, play, and exhibit far more joy than the average adult. They have a natural transparency to truth, beauty, and goodness. But after much disappointment, suffering, and adult conditioning, children tend to lose contact with their souls, and their capacity for curiosity and joy diminish greatly. Ironically, an infallible sign of spiritual maturity is the return of childlike qualities. This is why saints and mystics are typically the happiest people on the planet. Today, refrain from taking yourself too seriously. Choose to notice beauty and goodness wherever it arises, and remember to laugh.

**God my parent, help me
remember how to play.**

I Am a Child of God
July 21

"Blessed are the pure in heart, for they shall see God."
Jesus

It is hard to define purity, but we know it when we see it. When I first met Swami Nirvanandanda, our Italian swami, I knew I was in the presence of purity. His eyes were clear; his smile, genuine; his presence, warm; his words, sincere; and his soul, translucent. As I have gotten to know him over the years, I have even more respect for the depth of his purity. Though Swami Nirvanananda is wise, grounded, and very principled, he is simultaneously unassuming, simple, and very childlike. He plays and laughs often. What does this mean for you and me? We can't achieve a state of purity through our own willpower. An attribute of the soul, purity arises only when we no longer depend on our own cunning, control, or manipulation to feel safe. Purity is the natural fruit of trusting God's goodness, love, and protection. Communion with God liberates us to be who we actually are. Every time we pray or meditate, layers of psychological defenses fall away, and our innate purity effortlessly shines forth as simple, unadorned light.

**Allow me the freedom
of complete trust in you.**

Craig Bullock

I Am a Child of God

July 22

"Be as innocent as doves and wise as serpents."
Jesus

Early on in the development of the Franciscan Order, the bishop of Assisi closed down Francis' entire operation. Being humble of spirit, Francis did not protest. He did, however, go to Rome to ask permission to live out what Jesus had envisioned for him and his followers. In his meeting with Pope Innocent III, the pope asked Francis challenging questions about the difficult lifestyle he and his followers were attempting to live. Meekly, Francis paraphrased the words of Christ: "Look at the birds of the air; they neither sow nor reap, and yet our heavenly Father feeds them. Will he not feed us also?" The pope was so moved that he immediately gave permission for Francis and his followers to pursue their radical way of life. Turning to one of his cardinals, Pope Innocent observed, "We have made so much of original sin that we have forgotten about original innocence. That little beggar from Assisi embodies original innocence." For us, spiritual maturity is always a return to our original innocence.

**Beloved, you always see
my original innocence.**

Living Grace

I Am a Child of God
July 23

"If something is complicated, God is not in it."
Saint Francis of Assisi

Many years ago, I had the privilege of spending time with an individual I considered to be enlightened. At the end of our conversation, he asked if I had any questions. Of course, I asked him a rather complicated, philosophically oriented question. He replied, "Don't go crazy; keep it simple." Children are, generally speaking, simple. When asked a question they give honest answers. When they are happy, they smile; when they are sad, they cry; and when they are hungry, they eat. Their lives are organized around simple pursuits: play, curiosity and wonder. Jesus tells us that the kingdom of God is in our midst. Jesus means that all that we need to live fully and freely is available at all times. But it comes at a cost: we must be willing to surrender our complexity at the feet of God's simplicity. This surrender is not necessarily easy because complexity is seductive; it makes us feel important, in charge, and safe. One simple question continually confronts all of us: do we want to be complicated, or do we want to be happy?

God and guru, help me to surrender my complexity to the safety of your simplicity.

Craig Bullock

I Am a Child of God

July 24

"If God be for you, who can be against you?"
Saint Paul

Between the ages of twelve and sixteen, I essentially raised myself. Though I relished my freedom, I often felt overwhelmed by the task of taking care of myself. The summer before my junior year in high school, a priest arranged for me to live with a wonderfully loving and solid foster family. After a period of adjustment, a sense of lightness began to envelop me. I no longer had to worry about a roof over my head, food on the table, or making important life decisions all by myself. I could rest in the love and strength of my foster parents. They took care of life's business for me, so that I could be an adolescent. Likewise, all of our lives unfold within the context of God's wisdom, love, and protection. We are first and foremost God's beloved children and only secondly adults. Everything we have comes from God, including our abilities to plan, to work, to love, to create, and to provide for ourselves. God, who is both father and mother, has gifted us with everything that we need to live happy and dignified lives. No matter where we are or what we are doing, we always have God's full attention and provision. We just have to be willing, once again, to embrace our status as children of God in order to experience true freedom.

I always have your full attention and provision.

Living Grace

I Am a Child of God
July 25

"Whosoever therefore shall humble himself as this little child, the same is the greatest in the kingdom of heaven."
Jesus

Healthy children, secure in their parents' love, are rarely self-absorbed. Typically, they have no self-image to protect, no position to defend, and nothing to prove. They express their God-given gifts with hardly a thought of themselves. God's life just flows in and through them. As our hearts expand into God's infinitely loving heart, we too become less and less self-conscious. We are too busy living life, loving others, creating, and serving God to put a lot of thought and energy into ourselves or our performances. We show up for life without rigid agendas because we trust the flow of God's guidance and our own intuitive capacities. We stop worrying about the afterlife because we know it will be a continuation of our present life, only fuller and more expansive. We take no credit for our accomplishments because we understand that God is actually the doer, that God is manifesting the divine life in us and through us. As we come full circle, we define ourselves not by the standards of the world, but by our status as God's children.

**Beloved Mother God,
what do you wish for me today?**

Craig Bullock

I Am a Child of God

July 26

"God saw what He had created, and declared it good."
The Book of Genesis

On Thursday nights at the Assisi Institute, we host a meditation service that draws anywhere from 60 to 80 people. About halfway through the service we go into a period of silent meditation. And occasionally, I cheat. When I am supposed to be meditating myself, I open my eyes and watch people while they are meditating. What I see is absolutely breathtaking. I see people who love God. I see people's goodness, radiance, innocence, and beauty. I see God's light shining in and through everyone. I see God. Often I think to myself, this must be how God sees us all the time. He sees our beauty, our radiance and our potential for good. When God sees us, He sees His own luminous and unspeakable image. Now just imagine if we could see ourselves and others as God sees us. Imagine how free we would feel, how differently we would treat others, and how differently we would treat ourselves. To see as God sees is to catch a glimpse of heaven. Today, choose to see others and yourself through the eyes of God, as living manifestations of the divine life. This is what it means to be a child of God.

**Be thou my vision,
O Lord of my heart.**

The Guru

July 27

"The shepherd goes before the sheep and the sheep follow him."
Jesus

In the form of an avatar or an enlightened sage, God is perpetually becoming human, touchable, and personal. If God's love is to be actualized in our lives, we too must be human, touchable, and personal. If we cannot be psychologically vulnerable and transparent with at least one other human being, then our relationship with God is nothing more than a head trip, an illusion. In the same way, if we are unwilling to let go of ourselves in the service of someone or something, neither can we let go to God. Gurus and saints facilitate our surrender to God while never fashioning us into weak, dependent automatons. These holy ones serve us by liberating us from our self-imposed limitations and revealing our spiritual potential – truly a gift beyond measure.

Divine Mother, thank you for the holy ones you have sent to bring us home.

The Guru

July 28

"I have not come to bring peace on the earth; I have not come to bring peace, but a sword."
Jesus in the Gospel of Matthew, 10:34

Through the course of history, God has blessed us with enlightened visionaries. We canonize them, celebrate them, and name holidays after them. We make them user-friendly and domesticate them. We create or alter their images to make them look like us. In these ways, we effectively strip them of their power to challenge us, transform us, and bring us to new levels of freedom. Richard Rohr once said, "If the words of Jesus do not periodically make you uncomfortable, then you are not listening." This is why we must approach the great saints and gurus with a beginner's mind, letting go of what we think we know in order to experience our God-given potential. Authentic freedom does not come to us via the court of public opinion or psychological analysis, but by the sword of truth: God's unsettling but liberating wisdom.

**Guruji, I desire to let go of everything
I think I know in order to truly listen to you.**

The Guru
July 29

"I am the Good Shepherd. I know my own, and they know me."
Jesus

In the Good Shepherd, Jesus gives us a beautifully insightful metaphor of the guru-disciple relationship. The guru is like a shepherd who searches for you and me, the lost sheep. Upon finding a lost sheep, the shepherd lovingly places it upon his or her shoulders and carries it back to safety. The sheep, however, must agree to be carried. When we have committed ourselves to the guru, the burden of our lives belongs entirely to him or her. We must do our part to cooperate with the guru, but we are no longer in charge of the results. We no longer give God commands. With the faith of an innocent child, we accept whatever God and guru bring to us and no longer take comfort in our own strength or wisdom. Jesus said, "Be comforted, for I have overcome the world."

Victory to the guru! Jai guru!

Craig Bullock

Perpetually in God

July 30

"Be in contact with the infinite intelligence that is able to guide you and solve all problems."
Yogananda

The loving and providential wisdom of God is attempting to guide us in all our affairs. We can go a long way towards attuning ourselves to God's voice by using simple, unadorned common sense.

Common sense, however, is not as common as one might think. Our desires, preferences, and aversions keep us from clearly seeing the path we should take. Often, we want what we want instead of wanting the truth. Prayerful silence, humility, and a willingness to accept life on life's terms paves the way for clear sightedness. When we approach life with faith in God's goodness and an unprejudiced eye, the course of action we need to take naturally bubbles up into our awareness as inspired common sense, the fruit of which is almost always a sense of personal peace.

**I wait in confident anticipation
for your inspiration.**

Perpetually in God

July 31

"Our Father who art in heaven...thy will be done on earth as it is in heaven."
Jesus

When we make pronouncements about God we should do so with great humility. Human language and logic are utterly incapable of capturing the mystery of the Divine Life. So I offer this thought humbly: God needs us. Now, God does not need us to exist or in order to be complete! But God, with infinite wisdom, established life on planet Earth as a partnership between God and us. Therefore, God can only infuse our individual and collective lives with His beauty, goodness, and wisdom to the extent that we allow it. So in order for heaven to be unleashed on earth, our cooperation is absolutely needed. God needs our "Yes!" Have you realized how much faith God has in you? Nothing is more important or impactful to your life and the lives of others than your yes or no to God's love.

Beloved God, yes!

Holy Thinking

August 1

"Happiness depends chiefly on mental attitudes."
Yogananda

An attitude is a strong thought, feeling, or judgment. At a deeper level, an attitude is an entrenched stance towards ourselves, life, and God. As such, attitudes have the power to determine the quality of our lives. Negative attitudes clog our spiritual and creative arteries and prevent God's grace from flowing into our lives. A positive attitude is more than mere optimism; it is a reflection of a higher truth and a higher consciousness. An attitude that blesses us is a reflection of God's thoughts. The good news is that we have the ability to choose our attitudes at each and every moment of our lives. The process is simple: stop, breathe, and put all habitual and negative attitudes on hold. Through praying, chanting a mantra, or reading the words of a saint, lift your mind and heart towards God. A God-inspired attitude elevates us above fear and pessimism and infuses our minds with the light of truth, beauty, and goodness.

**Remind me that
my attitudes are choices.**

Holy Thinking
August 2

"Sincerity is a soul quality that God has given to every human being, but not all express it."
Yogananda

Sincerity is a powerful attitude which literally has the power to move heaven and earth. To understand sincerity, we must be clear about the distinction between the soul and the mind. The mind is a relatively superficial aspect of the human person. It is little more than a recording device which brings nothing new, fresh, or inspiring to our lives. Conversely, the soul is a pure reflection of God. Soulful thoughts, words, and feelings drip with authenticity, honesty, conviction, truth, purpose, power, and goodness. Sincerity is the soul's light bubbling up into our awareness, flooding our lives with divine possibilities. When we want God's transforming grace in our lives, we must endeavor to speak and act from a place of absolute sincerity. Yogananda teaches us, "Words saturated with sincerity, conviction, faith, and intuition are like highly explosive vibration bombs which, when set off, shatter the rocks of difficulties and create the change desired."

Beloved, give me the courage to speak and act with sincerity.

Holy Thinking

August 3

"You need not drown in the river of life when you encounter the strong storms of trials. Learn to be an expert boatman, and you can row across this tumultuous river to the safe shores of God."
Yogananda

Whenever we set out to do something worthwhile, rest assured that you will encounter opposing forces. These forces take the form of our own mental and bodily resistance, people invested in our stagnation, or spiritual principalities. An attitude of endurance is essential to success. Endurance is more than willful stubbornness; it is a heavenly energy, a fruit of the Holy Spirit. We must nurture endurance. Within the context of prayerful silence we must not shun the unpleasantness of resistance; we must bear discomfort calmly with faith in God's fidelity. When our lower nature fights our higher aspirations, we must not indulge or sanction it. As we keep our eyes steadily on the goal, the lower nature will lose force and power over time. Surrendering ourselves and our circumstances to God's loving providence will keep us firm and steady and help us to take both success and failure in stride.

**Endurance is heavenly energy,
your energy.**

Holy Thinking
August 4

"Change your thoughts if you wish to change your circumstances. Since you alone are responsible for your thoughts, only you can change them... Be a smile millionaire."
Yogananda

A stubbornly negative or dark stance blocks God's blessings; therefore, we must be willing to nurture a cheerful attitude. A cheerful attitude is not wishful thinking. Authentic cheerfulness is rooted in the truth that God's love is the most powerful force in all creation. Therefore, cheerfulness flows from our conscious choice to place our attention on God's all-powerful love. We must avoid the temptation to sit in sackcloth and ashes, to look and feel glum, to lament our failures, and to feel sorry for ourselves. Dark and hostile spiritual forces rejoice when we sink into the depths of depression. Out of your prayerful silence, laugh at your enemies, smile at your challenges, and rejoice in God's faithful goodness. Mother Meera, a spiritual companion of Sri Aurobindo, says, "A laugh of self-confidence and of faith in the Divine is the most shattering strength possible. It disrupts the enemy's front, spreads havoc in his ranks, and carries you triumphantly onwards."

Your love is the most powerful force in all of creation.

Holy Thinking

August 5

"He who speaks it knows it not, and he who knows it speaks it not."
Yogananda

If we want to remain in the flow of God's truth, beauty, and goodness, we must continually cultivate a beginner's mind. We must let go of all that we think we know. Emptiness is always the precondition for the experience of wisdom. For this reason, meditative silence is essential to the spiritual life. Such silence silences our raucous opinions, our unsettling preoccupations, and our noisy desires. True spirituality is never the path of addition but rather of subtraction, of letting go, of childlike simplicity. Rather than trying to acquire anything from God today, be content to know nothing, have nothing, and just be. In this way, the Spirit will fill you, bless you, and guide you in all of your affairs.

God, save me and others when I think I am wrong, and even more when I think I am right.

Facing Our Pain

August 6

"Blessed are they that mourn, for they shall be comforted."
Jesus

All of us have unconscious pockets of fear, hurt, and dread. The pursuit of spiritual peace does not make them disappear completely. Sooner or later, they emerge into our awareness. We must face our pain with a backdrop of silence and faith. Facing pain, though, has nothing to do with analysis, explanation, blaming, or storytelling. With the eye of our souls steadfastly fixed on God, we simply allow the pain to be present. Sometimes a helpful insight will spontaneously arise, and sometimes not. Of prime importance is our choice to keep our hearts open to the love of God and good friends. Prayer always helps. Sooner or later the pain will stop, and God's peace will effortlessly bubble up into our awareness. The pain may return, but with less sway over us. While I never want to glorify or romanticize suffering, my own experience tells me that God is present in our pain, and God uses it to open our hearts to greater and greater levels of peace, joy, and love.

**Beloved God, when my pain comes –
as it will – be with me.**

Craig Bullock

Facing Our Pain

August 7

"So be not the servant of the body or the mind… rise above all mental sensitivity and make yourself truly and everlastingly happy."
Yogananda

God never intended for our minds to cause us suffering, but they do. We often worry about future calamities that seldom materialize; we obsess about our imperfections to the point of self-hatred; we incessantly focus on images that disturb our peace; we get stuck in the past or the future; we fixate on our stories; and we get lost in our resentments. Then we spend enormous amounts of time, energy, and money trying to fix our minds, and our fixes do not work. In truth, we cannot fix the mind with the mind, any more than we can clean oil with oil. Something bigger and more powerful must intervene. One night many years ago I found myself awash in self-hatred. I tried spouting a few affirmations to no avail. Finally I simply sat in front of a picture of Yogananda and focused my gaze on his eyes while I mentally chanted, "God, Christ, Guru" with as much devotion as I could muster. After about thirty minutes, the self-incriminating voices fell silent, and only God's peaceful presence remained. God's grace prevailed over my mind.

**My God, I cannot fix my mind,
but you can.**

Living Grace

Facing Our Pain

August 8

"Jesus was led by the Spirit into the desert to be tempted."
The Gospel of Matthew

We have all inflicted suffering onto others, intentionally or accidentally. When we become aware of what we have done to others, we come face to face with our potential for meanness, selfishness, and pettiness. Believe it or not, these moments of self-discovery are essential to a loving, wholesome life, because until we come to terms with our potential for harm, we will repeat our destructive actions again and again. Facing our interior shadows gives birth to humility, compassion, grace, and wisdom. Whatever is brought into the light of God's consciousness and our consciousness has no power over us at all. This is why Jesus said, "You shall know the truth, and the truth will set you free."

**Beloved God, show me the truth
about my shadows.**

Facing Our Pain

August 9

"God's plan for creation is rooted only in love."
Yogananda

We are one with God's love, bigness, and strength; in fact, our lives are a participation in all that God is. The fruit of the experience of "participatory oneness" is that we are liberated to be more awake, honest, and present. We neither fear pain nor resist legitimate suffering. As our spirits ripen, we know that our lives are unfolding within the context of God's loving designs. Therefore, we are free to embrace the truth even when it is uncomfortable. We stop judging pain as "bad" because we know that pain is a most excellent teacher. Finally, we are liberated to embrace our suffering and the suffering of others because we know that all suffering is temporary, and God's love, joy, and goodness are eternal.

Teach me to face my pain and suffering instead of running from it.

Jesus
August 10

"Jesus Christ is very much alive and active today. In Spirit and occasionally taking on a flesh and blood form, he is working on behalf of the masses for the regeneration of the world."
Yogananda

God has only one desire: to pour out the entirety of His love onto humanity in a form that we can know, experience, taste, and touch. Jesus of Nazareth, fully human, a pious Jew and a mystic, was and is a full manifestation of God's love. His will, mind, strength, imagination, and spirit are entirely transparent to God's ineffable love, wisdom, and will. Jesus fully embodies God's consciousness, as does any true avatar. Jesus never said, "Worship me." He did say, "Follow me." He asks us to love him, so that we too can become more and more transparent to God's truth, beauty, and goodness. Today, prayerfully lift your mind and heart to Christ, and keep doing so until you experience Him lifting you out of darkness, fear, isolation, addiction, or hopelessness, and into the Divine Life.

Divine Mother, you sent Jesus for all of us.

Jesus

August 11

"And Jesus increased in wisdom and stature and in favor with God and man."
The Gospel of Luke

Jesus was and is an avatar, a Divine Incarnation. He entered the world with a "store of divine realization," according to Yogananda, and his consciousness was inseparable from God's consciousness. But Jesus, like us, had to develop and blossom over time. He had to learn from his parents, sit at the feet of enlightened Jewish teachers, and avail himself of the wisdom of India. Jesus' inherent divinity blossomed just as ours does: through joy and suffering, prayer and meditation, ecstatic moments and ordinary days. The lesson for us is clear: the spiritual life is never an escape from our humanness. Rather, it is the marriage of God's divinity with our humanity. Our spiritual life unfolds on the canvas of time, colored by all of our circumstances, and completed by the brush of the master painter. What is required of us is patience, faith in God's providence, humility, and the willingness to take an occasional, prayerful risk.

**Jesus, give me patience
on my journey.**

Jesus

August 12

"I have not come to abolish the law, but to fulfill it."
Jesus

Judaism is not a theoretical, philosophical, or worldly religion. It is life-centered, relationship-centered, and always God-centered. For Jews, God is not an impersonal cosmic force, but the ever present Breath of Life that sustains everyone and every living thing. Jesus was not the first Christian; he was a Jewish mystic. His mission was not to repudiate the God of Israel or the Jewish faith tradition. Jesus came to his people to call them and us to the authentic practice of religion: love, mercy, justice, compassion, and intimacy with God. For Jesus, God was neither a distant deity nor a stern judge, but "Abba," which means "Papa," and even "Mama." Jesus came to us not to claim a special relationship to God, but to call the entire world into relationship with the God of Love.

**Jesus, you invite me to know
the Divine Mother as you know Her.**

Jesus

August 13

"Hear O' Israel, the Lord our God, the Lord is One."
Shema Yisrael

Jesus belongs to everyone, and his message and mission are a blessing to the entire world. The resurrection is not, therefore, an esoteric belief. Rather, the resurrection is the invasion of the fire of God's love into the lifeless body of Jesus and also into the very fabric of the human condition. At the resurrection event, a Divine Energy was released into creation that is capable of elevating us above our darkest and most destructive tendencies. This Energy, the very Breath or Spirit of God, is pure, powerful, and palpable. For Jesus, there were no outsiders. Everyone belonged, everyone was called to the heavenly banquet, and everyone was a child of God: mother, father, brother, sister, family, and friend. The resurrection is available to all humble and earnest people of goodwill, regardless of their religious affiliation. The only requirement for receiving the grace of the resurrection is that we allow this heavenly fire to increasingly take possession of our lives.

**Jesus, resurrect me
and the entire world.**

Living Grace

Healing
August 14

"The greatest learning of the ages lies in accepting life exactly as it comes to us."
Father Anthony de Mello

Because we live in a culture that pretends to have a "fix" for everything that ails us, many of us have fallen into the trap of endlessly trying to fix ourselves. This is a form of madness because it never really works. Additionally, our obsession with fixing our flaws keeps our attention on ourselves, not God. Paradoxically, true healing begins with acceptance of God's complete, unconditional acceptance of ourselves. Then healing can begin: acceptance begets stillness; stillness begets peace; and peace begets healing. Healing has nothing to do with fixing! It is the natural expansion of our awareness into the experience of God-union. When in doubt, resist nothing and accept everything – especially yourself.

God, you completely accept me just as I am. Now, may I accept myself in the same way.

Healing

August 15

"A leper came to Jesus, imploring him."
The Gospel of Mark

Most of us have had the feeling of being an outcast, alienated from God and those we love, and full of shame. Shame is the profoundly toxic experience of feeling less than others, defective, and broken. Shame causes us to constrict emotionally, socially, and spiritually, and to hide from God and others. In Jesus' time, lepers were excluded from community life. Lepers were required to shout, "Stay away; I am unclean!" One leper, however, dared to approach Jesus and ask for a healing. He must have known that Jesus was different, that he welcomed everyone, regardless of illness, social status, gender, or sins. What was true for the leper is true for us: no matter what we have done, no matter how inadequate we feel, Jesus says to us, "Don't hide. Don't stay away. Pray, meditate, and come home! All is forgiven! I long for your company."

**Jesus, Son of David,
have mercy on me.**

Healing

August 16

"A leper came to Jesus imploring him, and kneeling, said to him, 'If you will, you can make me clean.'"
The Gospel of Mark

Like the leper in the gospel narrative, we are all in need of healing. Some of us deny that we need healing; some of us do not believe that we can be healed, and some of us seek healing in all the wrong places. The leper gives us a timeless roadmap to the healing process. He does not ask why he is ill. He does not blame himself for his condition. He does not read self-help books. He does not spend years in therapy to analyze the cause of his illness. He seeks the help of a God-realized person, a power greater than himself, in a spirit of humility, vulnerability, and trust. Whenever we pray, meditate, reflect on the words of a saint, or turn to God for help, we give heaven permission to bless us with all that is good, all that will heal us.

Beloved God, stop me from doing those things which block my receptivity to healing.

Healing

August 17

"Moved with pity, Jesus stretched out his hand and touched him, and said, 'I am willing; be cleansed.'"
The Gospel of Mark

The leper in the gospel story was healed instantaneously. Sometimes this occurs for us, but most often the fulfillment of our desire for wholeness unfolds over many years – not because we are doing anything wrong, but because this is the path that God has chosen for us, and whatever path God chooses always serves our highest evolutionary growth. Waiting for healing requires dedication, perseverance, and endurance. It pulls from our hearts a depth of prayer, longing, and love for the Divine Beloved that is otherwise hidden beneath our more superficial desires. Such heartfelt depth is the exact salve necessary to heal our soul's incurable wounds and invisible pains. So if God does not appear to answer your desire for wholeness in a timely manner, do not lose heart. Follow your impulses for deep prayer and deep love, which is the very essence of healing and wholeness.

**Beloved, wait with me
as I wait for you.**

Healing

August 18

"The leprosy left him and he was made clean. He went out and began to talk freely about it, and people came to Jesus from every quarter."
The Gospel of Mark

The ultimate sign of the leper's healing was not his return to physical health, but his willingness to be of service to his guru, to Jesus. Focused on God and inspired by his experience, he took it upon himself to lead people to Jesus so that they too could be healed. Early on in Yogananda's ministry in the United States, he performed many healings. Over time, though, he healed less and less because he discovered that people certainly wanted a healing, but not the healer, God. A physical healing is good, but it does not last forever. We will all eventually die, but our conscious contact with God will echo throughout eternity. Even more, the choice to spend our lives in service of God and guru puts us in the direct flow of love, the most powerful force in all of creation. Thus, the opportunity to be a wounded healer and to serve the reunification of humankind to God is the greatest healing that we can ever have.

**Guruji, may I extend
your healing love to all.**

Happiness

August 19

"No one can be made happy unless he rises above himself...but we cannot rise above ourselves unless a higher power lifts us up."
Saint Bonaventure

As the very image of God, we exist to experience perfect happiness, the very same joy, peace, and love that God experiences. However, because most of us have forgotten our innate connection to God, we create happiness projects, looking for happiness in all the wrong places. We cannot give our happiness projects up until we catch a glimpse of a larger happiness. Enter the guru! Did you ever stop to think why Jesus, Francis, and Yogananda attracted so many followers? It was not due to the easy lives they offered their disciples. Yet countless disciples have followed them because they radiated profound bliss, truth, and love. In the presence of such exquisite happiness, devotees let go of their happiness projects entirely. As for us, we simply maintain conscious contact with the guru. Consistently hold an image of the guru in your mind's eye, and ask for help, wisdom, and a heart full of love. In time, the guru will elevate us out of our suffering and into heavenly joy.

**Oh my guru, may I live not
for my happiness projects, but for you.**

Happiness

August 20

"Your soul, being a reflection of the ever joyous Spirit, is happiness itself."
Yogananda

Part of the reason we think we lack happiness is that we tend to have a myopic, limited understanding of true happiness. We tend to reduce happiness to a sense of inner delight, joy, or pleasantness. Happiness can be so much more! Consider these: contentment, peace, alertness, calmness, creativity, expansiveness, clarity, interior silence, compassion, empathy, discipline, strength, endurance, wisdom, truth, security, playfulness, lightness, equanimity, acceptance, surrender, trust, faith, hope, and love. These shades of happiness bubble up into our awareness to the extent that we enter into the Great Silence, sit at the feet of the guru, and seek to be a channel of God's love.

Beloved God, help me to understand what happiness really means.

Happiness

August 21

"He who seeks to gain his life will lose it, and he who seeks to lose his life, for my sake, will gain it."
Jesus

We live in a culture that makes experience itself the goal of life. Isn't much of what we do based on how we think it will make us feel? Do we not judge the value of something by whether or not it brings us pleasure? Pleasure has become society's highest value. Pleasure can be bought and sold, because pleasure is the enjoyment of an object – like a piece of candy. Happiness, though, is not an object; it can be experienced, but never possessed. When we make happiness the goal of our lives, it remains elusive. But the spiritual life offers us a very different roadmap: a life lived not for happy experiences, but a life filled with truth, compassion, love, and service. Paradoxically, these spiritual values effortlessly yield a harvest of soulful happiness. So never chase the experience of happiness. Just do good, be good, and serve the highest good of others, and you will have more happiness than you can possibly handle.

**My goal is not happiness;
my goal is love.**

Courage

August 22

"Behold, I am with you always, until the end of the age."
Jesus

Without courage, it is not possible to live a full, creative, and spiritual life. Courage is not machismo, the absence of fearful feelings, or the denial of danger. Courage means that our fearful reactions do not overshadow our willingness to pursue the truth or to press on with our God-inspired purposes. If we want to be fully alive and self-realized, we have to accept the fact that we will experience moments of profound insecurity. We must be willing to cross these thresholds of anxiety in spite of how they make us feel. Authentic courage is always a participation in God's courage. Did it not take God tremendous courage to create the human race, to give us free will, and to place planet Earth in our hands? Simply put, courage is a Divine Force that empowers us to do what is beyond our natural inclinations. Our job is simple: to continuously place our gaze on the guru, surrendering our cares and our lives into God's hands. Then we must choose to act on the inspirations that come to us, which in turn opens us to an even deeper flow of Divine Energy.

God, you hold all the courage I will ever need at the ready.

Courage

August 23

"Take courage! I am here."
Jesus

Everyone reading these words is already courageous. Your soul chose to incarnate on planet Earth, and you continue to remain here in spite of all of your life's challenges. Courage is not born of stubborn willpower, but of a love for truth, beauty, and goodness. Your soul chose to come to planet Earth because you wanted to be a vehicle for Divinity and part of humankind's regeneration. We grow and deepen our capacity for courage not by the denial of danger, insecurity, or fear, but by our willingness to listen to God's voice in the depths of our souls. God gives us strength and empowers us to press boldly forward, regardless of the dangers that confront us. Meditative silence is the opening by which we are infused with the very courage of God. So embrace your deeper intuitions, your finer aspirations, and those heavenly inspirations that come to you in the dark of night. Yogananda said, "Many people come to me to talk about their worries. I urge them to sit quietly, meditate, and pray, and after feeling that calmness within, to think of alternative ways by which the problem can be eliminated."

Beloved, may I believe that I am courageous simply because I am here.

Courage
August 24

"We know the love that God has for us, and we trust that love."
The First Letter of John

By the very fact that you are on a spiritual path, you are endeavoring to resurrect your soul to its rightful place in your life; that is, you are attempting to live from your deepest depths instead of from your surface personality. You cannot do this, however, without periodically undergoing periods of anxiety. Following the intuitive guidance of your soul necessarily creates anxiety because it takes you out of your comfort zone, pushes you beyond your survival strategies, and challenges your stories about God and yourself. A degree of anxiety is, therefore, often a sign – not that you are doing things wrong, but that you are doing things right. Like Yogananda, you and I need human support and the support that comes with prayer and meditation. Authentic self-realization is, paradoxically, a communal effort. We need God and we need each other. Reflecting on the importance of spiritual friendship, Yogananda wrote: "True friendship consists in being mutually useful in offering one's friend good cheer in distress, sympathy in sorrow, and material help in time of real need."

God, show me who you have sent to be my spiritual friends.

Courage

August 25

"We love because he first loved us."
The First Letter of John

A charming but challenging episode from the life of St. Francis perfectly captures the essence of spiritual courage. Francis' father dragged him before the bishop and people of Assisi to publically condemn him for his new found spirituality and his generosity towards the poor. His father even ridiculed Francis for wearing the clothes he had given him. What did Francis do? He stripped naked in front of everyone and handed his clothes back to his father, announcing, "From this day forward, God is my Father." Francis' symbolic act was both outrageously courageous and lovingly vulnerable. Spirituality demands courage because spirituality means being so absolutely present that we disappear. Courage is actually God's voice telling us that it is safe to be naked, to let go, to be our real selves. Courage is the willingness to open wide the doors of our souls, to be who God intended us to be – no matter how uncomfortable that is at some moments. Courage is the willingness to trust God's wisdom. More than anything else, courage is the triumph of love over fear.

**Courage is the triumph
of love over fear.**

Courage
August 26

"Not even a sparrow falls to the ground outside the Father's care."
The Gospel of Matthew

Yogananda experienced many intense trials during his early years in the United States. So great were his problems that at one point he retreated to Mexico and seriously considered abandoning his mission. While in prayerful meditation, however, he heard the Divine Mother say to him, "Go back." And he obeyed! We must always remember that the spiritual life is neither an escape into nirvana nor a type of retirement home for mystics. The spiritual path is a full-fledged adventure, abounding in all sorts of dangers, challenges, and rewards. God does not want to lull us into a state of blissful dullness. Rather, God wants to expand our capacity to be conduits for truth, beauty, and goodness, to be His irrepressible song in the drama of creation. Therefore, courage is a necessity in the spiritual life. What is courage? Courage is being so surrendered to God's loving providence that we allow His energy to sustain us, to embolden us, and to propel us forward, no matter how daunting the obstacles might be.

God, help me to remember that my life with you is not meant to be nirvana, but an adventure.

Craig Bullock

Surrender

August 27

"Unless the grain of wheat falls to the ground and dies, it remains just a grain of wheat. But if it dies, it produces much fruit."
Jesus

God is everything that is true, good, and beautiful – beyond our wildest imaginations. We have been loved into existence not to lead lives of quiet desperation, but to be ever-expanding expressions of God. God wants to show up in and through you, as you. Now that is a life worth living! How does such a thing happen? Not by conquering a spiritual version of Mount Everest. Rather, God increases in us to the extent that we let go of ourselves. This means letting go of our agendas, positions, demands, plans, and maps of how we want our lives to unfold. It means saying "yes" to God and guru – whether or not situations make sense to us. It means learning to die before we die, so that the Divine Life can bubble up within us, with increasing intensity, here and now.

Do I dare to believe that you, Beloved God, want to live a life as me?

Surrender

August 28

"God is the nearest of the near, dearest of the dear, closer than the closest."
Yogananda

God is entirely good and all-powerful. Therefore, if we have abandoned ourselves entirely to God's loving goodness, what do we have to fear? Nothing!

But we humans do not abandon ourselves instinctively. In order to feel safe, we place ourselves at the center of our lives, secure behind a wall of our fears, desires, assumptions, beliefs, and judgments. In effect, we tell God how things should be, attempting to fashion God into our own image and likeness. Of course, this method of living is a recipe for an insufferable life because it places too much of the burden for our lives on us. We have not been created to handle our lives on our own, but to live them in and with God. Today, try an experiment. Assume that everything that comes to you, including painful or uncomfortable experiences, has been designed by God, the Master Architect, to serve your highest evolutionary transformation. Let your prayers be, "As you wish; what is your lesson for me?" or, "What would you have me do in this situation?" Two things are likely to happen: you will be filled with peace, and you will receive answers to your prayers.

As you wish.

Surrender

August 29

"I praise you God because I am wonderfully made... in my mother's womb you knit me together."
Psalm 139

A liberating and beautiful fruit of surrender is self-acceptance. Each one of us has been created by God, knit together by the loving wisdom of the Divine Mother. We are not accidents, but the handiwork of God who reflects a unique aspect of God. This means that even our limitations, clumsiness, and foibles are part of the plan. God works for our transformation even through our most regrettable actions. What a relief! But self-acceptance is not mindlessly giving in to self-indulgence, in which we allow all of our addictions and negative tendencies to run rampant. Self-acceptance is being compassionately conscious of all aspects of our personalities, including our most undesirable traits, and surrendering them to a God who is the very essence of tender mercy. When surrendered to God, our imperfections and failures become portals to God's wondrous grace.

Beloved God, you will weave each and every part of me – past, present, and future – into your Divine Image.

Surrender

August 30

"Sometimes, when the Mother is going to caress you, a shadow is caused by Her hand before it touches you. So when trouble comes, don't think She is punishing you; Her hand overshadowing you holds some blessing as it reaches out to bring you nearer to Her."
Yogananda

External events do not cause stress; it is our reaction to these events that puts us into a state of discomfort. Imagine how peaceful we would be if we just assumed that everything comes to us from God in order to serve our highest good! Yet I am not suggesting passivity in the face of life's challenges. Rather, I am saying that if we resist nothing and accept everything as part of a divine plan, we will maintain a sense of calmness in all circumstances. From this place of calmness, we will intuitively know what needs to be done. Surrender is indeed a blow to our false sense of autonomy and personal power. Yet the simple prayer, "Thy will be done" is the only way to interior peace and true freedom.

**Divine Mother, you wish only
to love and bless me, even if all I can see
is the shadow of your hand.**

Craig Bullock

Surrender

August 31

"We are continuously immersed in God's merciful grace like the air that permeates us."
Father Solanus Casey

The life of Father Solanus Casey, a Franciscan priest who died in 1957, offers a wonderful example of spiritual surrender. Just before he was ordained, he was told that he would be allowed to say mass but not to hear confessions because he was not smart enough. Because of his intellectual limitations, the new priest was given the job of answering the parish doorbell. Father Casey did not resist his humble role. Often, when people would come to the parish in dire need, he was the one to greet them. They would tell him their problems, and he listened with loving compassion and offered to pray for them. Not only did people feel the peace of God after talking to Father Casey, but ultimately they reported that their prayers had been answered. Miraculous healings became commonplace. Hundreds gathered each day to ask for his prayers. Always, he said, "Yes." As he lay dying, his last words were, "I give my soul to Jesus Christ." Over twenty thousand people attended his funeral. When they exhumed his body thirty years later, it was incorrupt. All of this happened because he surrendered to the will of God over and over. Such is the power of surrender!

Nothing can limit your loving design for my life.

Moods

September 1

"God is managing the whole universe, down to the most minute detail – and we are made in His image."
Yogananda

Yogananda states, "Moods are not easily defined; but you know what they are. When you are in a mood, your behavior is not natural. You are not the person you should be. The end result is that you feel wretched." After prayer and meditation, nothing is more important in the management of moods than the ability to observe our thoughts and feelings and to understand what triggers our moodiness. I am not referring to the neurotic tendency to analyze and judge ourselves, but to our soul's capacity to compassionately witness the machinations of the mind. This is the bottom line: whatever we can stand back and observe has no power over us, including our moods. It is the soul that compassionately witnesses all events, and our souls are rooted in the eternal, in God. They are, therefore, always larger than our errant thoughts and distorted emotions. By grounding our awareness in our soul's capacity to compassionately witness what is going on in and around us, we resist drama and learn to trust God's loving providence.

Give me the grace to compassionately detach from my moods.

Moods

September 2

"When you are thinking creatively, you don't feel the body or moods; you become attuned with Spirit."
Yogananda

The best way to avoid negative moods is to begin the day with meditation, silence, and prayer. This time grounds our day in God's peaceful presence and energizes our will, thoughts, and emotions with heavenly inspiration. Next, as we move toward engaging the duties of the day, we must avoid doing so from a place of passivity or mindlessness. Yogananda says, "The time when your mind is vacant is just the time that it can become moody, and when you are moody, the devil comes in and wields his influence on you." The antidote to a passive or vacant mind is creative thinking. Get in the habit of asking yourself the following questions: What do I want to create today? What is the wisest response to this challenge? How can I enjoyably tackle this difficult task? How can I be a channel of God's light and love in this situation? When we choose to stay awake, when we alertly choose to live creatively, and when we actively invite God into the details of our lives, a light literally infuses our awareness with strength, clarity, and joy.

What can I create today?

Moods

September 3

"Fear is useless. What is needed is trust."
Jesus

My first meditation teacher used to tell me, "If you hang around a barber shop long enough, you are going to get a haircut. And if you hang around saints, sooner or later you will become a saint." The mind is like a mirror; it becomes the images that it focuses on. In other words, moodiness occurs when we allow our thoughts, emotions, and imaginations to be hijacked by negativity, most often in the form of fear or shame. Pretending that we don't feel fear and shame does not protect us from negative moods at all! What does elevate us above moodiness, however, is the choice to open our minds to truth, beauty, and goodness, to God. We become what we focus on, absorb, and digest. When we consistently enter into communion with God, our lives become a divine affair. Though our minds like to complicate the process, it is that simple!

I become what I love.

Moods

September 4

Pure Truth – which emanates from the mouths of great saints, sages, and small children – purifies the mind, expands the heart, and elevates the consciousness. Below, you will find some common emotions that pollute our thinking and the corresponding truths that act as a healing balm upon the mind.

Fear about the state of the world or our lives: *"God is managing everything, down to the most minute detail."* –Yogananda

Anger over being hurt by someone: *"Father, forgive them, for they know not what they do."* –Jesus

Shame or guilt over something we have done: *"God's very name is mercy."* –Pope Francis

Anxiety over life's important choices: *"Seek first the kingdom of God, and everything you need will be given unto you."* –Jesus

Overwhelmed by a challenge: *"If you have faith the size of a mustard seed, you will say to this mountain, 'Move from here to there,' and it will move; and nothing will be impossible to you."* –Jesus

Beloved, thank you for the unfailing gift of Pure Truth.

Living Grace

Yogananda

September 5

"The Good Shepherds of this world come down from their high places and give their lives to searching for disciples who are lost in darkness. They find them in desolate and dangerous places, arouse them, lift them to a divine shoulder, and bear them rejoicing to a safe place in the fold."
Yogananda

Yogananda did not create his own mission, and he never taught in his own name. Rather, he was chosen by God. When his parents took him to Lahiri Mahasaya for baptism, Lahiri prophesized that Yogananda would be "a spiritual engine who will carry many souls to God's kingdom." Yogananda himself explained his mission when he said, "To reestablish God in the temples of souls through the revival of the original teachings of God-communion as propounded by Christ and Krishna is why I was sent to the West." Yogananda's life has created saints, blessed countless devotees, and helped to create harmony between people of different faith traditions. The implication for us is clear: availing ourselves of Yogananda's teachings and guidance brings us into conscious contact with God's depthless love. Yogananda initiates his followers into the Divine Life and opens them to a life overflowing with truth, beauty, and goodness.

Dear God, thank you for Yogananda.

Yogananda

September 6

"The yogi learns to find God in the cave of his heart."
Yogananda

Yogananda teaches that moments of God-communion are meant to be a stabilized aspect of our consciousness, and even more, that God wants us to be in conscious contact with Him every moment of our lives! Here is one of Yogananda's favorite meditations: Sitting in a meditative posture, take your left hand and place it over your heart center; place your right hand over your left. Gently steady your breath. Holding a mental image of Christ or your guru, mentally say on your inhalation, "I am thine." Pause a second or two. With your exhalation, mentally say, "Thou art mine." Repeat this cycle fourteen times, each time pulling your awareness deeper and deeper in order to mentally touch the point behind your heart. Especially in the pause, feel the peace, stillness, and sweetness. Then, drop your hands and just rest in God's presence. After a few minutes, repeat the cycle. Finally, offer a prayer of gratitude to God and ask to be God's instrument of peace in the world. We only begin to be truly human when we prayerfully enter our own hearts. Welcome to your identity in God.

**I am thine;
thou art mine.**

Yogananda

September 7

"The yogi learns to find God in the cave of his heart."
Yogananda

If we are honest with ourselves, we will admit that the torturous activities of the ego bubble within. These include judgments, fears, obsessions, doubts, comparisons, unruly desires, and more. Ultimately, psychological analysis is incapable of stilling the ego's voice. For this reason, Yogananda directs us to dive deeper and deeper into the absolute peace of stillness. In stillness, we encounter God simply, directly, and purely, and in this encounter, the ego is incapable of creating drama, telling stories, or overwhelming us with waves of self-loathing. Each and every time we enter into the stillness, the ego's grip on our hearts and minds is weakened until it becomes a humble instrument of our soul's aspirations. Meditation allows us to maintain a zone of interior awareness, a point of calmness, as we engage the world. From this calmness, God's wisdom is available to guide us in all our affairs. Nothing is more practical than stillness.

**Make me an instrument
of your peace.**

Yogananda

September 8

"Stillness is God."
Yogananda

Generally speaking, the entire human race suffers from an anxiety disorder. We tend to see ourselves as isolated entities, distinct and separate from God and each other. This paradigm means that we are on our own; the managing of our lives is entirely up to us; everything is on our own shoulders alone; we alone make or break our destinies. And though the entire human race is tempted to cling to these illusions of control, they are completely wrong. This erroneous belief in our separateness is a recipe for a profound sense of inadequacy and a deep level of anxiety. Yogananda teaches that we are part and parcel of God, that we are as close to God as we will ever be, and that we only have to improve our knowing. Yogananda gives us more than an inspiring belief. He gives us an invitation to live our lives in conscious partnership with God. Do we have burdens to carry? For sure! However, we never carry them alone. God walks with us every step of our lives.

Divine Beloved, I will never be closer to you than I am at this very moment.

Living Grace

Perpetually in God

September 9

"God's divine power has given us everything we need for a godly life."
The Second Book of Peter

Albert Einstein made an insightful observation: "There are only two ways to live your life. One is as though nothing is a miracle. The other is as though everything is a miracle." We tend to reduce the miraculous only to displays of supernatural power. In reality, all life is miraculous; we just need to have our eyes opened. The fact that you and I are alive and self-aware is inexplicably miraculous. The deer presently grazing in my backyard are wondrously miraculous. The cup of coffee I am now sipping is pleasingly miraculous. The laughs that my wife and I will share today are delightfully miraculous. Even the pain we feel in grieving the loss of a loved one is miraculous because it reflects the miraculous bond of love. And nothing is more miraculous, more divine, than our capacity to show mercy, to forgive, to release someone from guilt. Life is miraculous because it is a participation in the one life, the Divine Life. Spirituality is simply about waking up to the presence of the miraculous in our day-to-day lives. Today, allow your life to be an expression of the miraculous: welcome God's mercy into your life by forgiving someone who has harmed you, and then forgive yourself.

Open my eyes to miracles.

Perpetually in God

September 10

"I have come that you might have life and life abundantly."
Jesus

Many years ago, I went to my spiritual director complaining that I was praying to God for guidance, but God was not responding. He answered, "You know, God is very busy. He has many responsibilities." I asked him if that meant that God was too busy to answer my prayers. He said, "No, but God is not going to waste time speaking to you if you are not going to listen to what He has to say." Simply put, God's miraculous love can only break into our lives to the degree that we are open to it, without conditions or qualifications. In other words, the willingness to obey God's guidance is the necessary precondition for receiving guidance. We are hesitant to be open and obedient because we fear what God might do. We believe that God wants to limit our happiness, when, in actuality, God's will is the only source of true happiness. Yogananda tells us that, "God is love; His plan for creation is rooted only in love." And he also says, "There is no other way to find God's love than to surrender to Him."

You know what I need, always.

Living Grace

Perpetually in God

September 11

"Thy kingdom come; thy will be done, on earth as it is in heaven."
Jesus

Growing up Catholic, I was encouraged to be practical and to be grounded in the physical world. At the same time, I was invited to participate in a reality that transcended the five senses and the limits of the logical mind. I was also told that the door between our world and the spiritual world was always open, that angels, saints, and departed loved ones are a part of our everyday life, and that heaven constantly serves our spiritual evolution. Do you know, for example, that when we meditate the angels are washing our feet and that the guru is literally blessing us? Do you know that God desires that we experience a living and conscious marriage between our world and the heavenly realms? Do you know that we become more human, more functional, and more alive to the extent that God's light permeates our consciousness? We are multi-dimensional beings. Therefore, if we want our lives and our world to be truly peaceful, we must take our cues from heaven's inspirations and allow heaven to serve us. We need the miraculous, that is, a higher power to make us whole and restore sanity to our lives.

**You serve me infinitely more
than I could ever hope to serve you.**

Craig Bullock

Perpetually in God

September 12

"Therefore, if any man be in Christ, he is a new creature. Old things are passed away; behold all things become new."
The Second Book of Corinthians

In college, I studied German. I became so frustrated with its complicated grammar and confusing word order that I went to my professor to complain. After a few minutes of my grumbling, he answered, "Do you want the German language to understand you or do you want to understand it?" I sheepishly told him that I wanted to understand German. He replied, "Then get beyond your whining and accept German for the complex and beautiful language that it is. Let the German language make you a German speaker rather than squeezing it into your English speaking mind." I needed a new attitude in order to learn German. Similarly, we often don't often recognize our moment-by-moment encounters with God because our instinct to is to force God into our usual categories, expectations, and politics. If an encounter with the Divine does not bring us to something new, then what value does it have? Our relationship with God is not about getting lost in tranquility or retreating into a spiritual shell; it is about becoming God-like.

**Let me not try to make you
into what I expect; make me into you.**

Perpetually in God

September 13

"For She (wisdom) is a breath of the power of God, and a pure emanation of the glory of the Almighty... For She is a reflection of eternal light."
The Book of Wisdom

We are perpetually in the stream of God's uncreated Light, or we would cease to exist. Spirituality is the ever-deepening process of becoming aware of God's Light and open to its inspiration. Every sincere prayer, every expression of true devotion, and every act of surrender immerses our consciousness in the river of Divine Light. Yogananda taught that the sound of Aum (OM) is the auditory manifestation of this Light. By chanting Aum with concentrated devotion and love, we become increasingly conscious of the power and presence of God's Light, experienced as whatever is needed in any given moment, from inner illumination, to peace, to strength, to love. As you go about fulfilling your responsibilities today, steady your breath, bring your awareness to your heart center, and mentally chant Aum. If you consistently repeat this simple practice, you will experience the opening of your heart along with a sense of God's presence. Chanting Aum makes us light bearers, instruments of the Holy Spirit.

Aum.

Perpetually in God

September 14

"God, the Father of all, vibrates through nature as the eternal life, and that life has the sound of the great Amen or Aum."
Yogananda

Sit comfortably in a chair; head, neck, and spine gently aligned. Steady your breath, pausing briefly between inhalation and exhalation. After a few minutes, bring your awareness to your right hand; be in your right hand, and continue to breathe rhythmically. Mentally chant Aum three or four times. Tighten your hand for a few seconds and then release. Do this two or three times. Feel the energy or life force vibrating within your hand, a sure manifestation of Aum. Then, while maintaining your rhythmic breathing, mentally repeat three or four times the following words: God is in my hand. Notice what you are experiencing, and enjoy the peaceful and enlivening vibration of Aum. Finally, place your hand over your heart and mentally repeat three or four times: God is within me. Stay alert, allowing yourself to merge with the enlivening presence of Spirit percolating within your body. Whenever your thoughts are running wild or you are emotionally agitated, come back to this simple but powerful meditation.

I am in God;
God is in me.

God Speaks

September 15

"Be still and know that I am God."
Psalm 46

In the Jewish scriptures, there is a wonderful story about God speaking to the prophet Elijah. God did not speak to Elijah in the ways we would expect, like an earthquake, a mighty wind, or a great fire. Rather, God spoke to Elijah in a gentle whisper. What was true for Elijah is true for us. God speaks to us, every moment of our existence, as a gentle whisper. God speaks! And because our DNA is Divine, we are all genetically programmed to hear God's voice. Only one question remains: Do we really want to hear what God has to say? Many will say that they desire to commune with God, but do they know what that implies? When God communicates with us, He does not merely pass on interesting information. Rather, God speaks to us in order to draw us into an intimate relationship with Himself. We all know that intimacy demands transparency, presence, and responsiveness. Hearing God's voice is the same as loving God, and loving God means that we are vulnerable: We are ready to give up our protective barriers; there are no closed doors or windows; we are holding nothing back; we are totally in.

Beloved, you will whisper to me in exactly the right way at exactly the right time.

God Speaks

September 16

"To know much and taste nothing – of what use is that?"
Saint Bonaventure

Recently, I spent time with my eight-month old grandson, Noah. We shared wondrous moments of laughter, baby-talk, and off-key singing. But the most precious moment happened when we silently gazed into each other's eyes. It was as if our souls were making contact beyond the medium of sounds, words, or concepts. I will never forget that moment of soulful recognition. What is true below is true above. In other words, thoughts, words, and concepts can convey a sliver of God's presence, but only deep silence can give us the direct experience of God. If it is pure and soulful contact with God that we desire, we must stand naked before the Divine Beloved; we must go beyond our beliefs, categories, and concepts; we must abandon language altogether. Silence is the language of God and everything else a poor translation.

**Dearest God, may our first
and foremost love language be silence.**

God Speaks
September 17

"My mother and brothers are those who hear God's word and put it into practice."
Jesus, from the Gospel of Luke, 8:21

God speaks to us most clearly in the guru – disciple relationship. We may encounter many inspiring teachers in a given lifetime, but there is only one guru. Yogananda tells us, "A true guru, ordained by God to help sincere seekers in response to their deep soul craving, is not an ordinary teacher: he is a human vehicle whose body, speech, mind, and spirituality God uses as a channel to attract and guide lost souls to their home of immortality." Simply put, the God–realized guru takes us by the hand and leads us back to God. Our job is to willingly sit at our guru's feet, allowing him or her to infuse us with wisdom and to saturate our hearts with God's grace. If you consider yourself a devout disciple of Jesus, I suggest that you only read the gospels for fifteen minutes a day for the next thirty days. If you are a devotee on the path of Kriya Yoga, I recommend you read only Yogananda's writings every day for the next month. This focused reading will allow the gurus' consciousness, their God-realization, to permeate your consciousness. Yogananda said, "When I am gone, the teachings will be the guru."

Oh my guru, come to me
and lead me home to God.

God Speaks

September 18

"In things of beauty, Francis contemplated the One who is supremely beautiful, and, led by the footprints he found in creatures, he followed the Beloved everywhere."
Saint Bonaventure

The physical universe is literally a scripture bearing the very footprints of God. In the sunrise, God says to us, "I gift you with another day, full of possibilities and blessings." In the food we eat, God says, "I am taking care of you, providing for you, loving you." In the air we breathe, God is saying, "I am sustaining you, enlivening you, and inspiring you." In the earth itself, God is saying, "I am holding you, grounding you, and securing you." In the beauty of flowers God is saying, "I am smiling at you and bestowing joy upon you." In every speck of creation God says to us, "I love you; I am with you; I am for you." Yogananda tells us that, "Spirit has expressed itself as the vast body of nature. I am the stars, I am the waves, I am the life of all, I am the laughter within all hearts, I am the smile on the faces of the flowers and in each soul. I am the wisdom and power that sustains all creation."

Divine Mother, may I hear your voice in all of creation.

God Speaks

September 19

"God is love; His plan for creation can be rooted only in love. Every saint who has penetrated to the core of reality has testified that a divine universal plan exists and that it is beautiful and full of joy."
Yogananda

God perpetually speaks to us. God gives us not words, but love. And this means that God is giving Himself because God is love. Love can, of course, can have many faces: gentleness, fierceness, stillness, passion, and so forth. We know we are hearing God because love melts the boundaries we place around ourselves and others and softens our hard edges. We know we are hearing God because enemies become more like friends. We know we are hearing God because we are less and less shackled by anxiety and fear. We know we are hearing God because we are more and more ourselves: the selves that have been hidden in God for all of eternity. We know we are hearing God because we are fully participating in life, and we are wholly present to our experiences, regardless if they are pleasant or painful. And we know we are hearing God because we are becoming more Godlike, irrespective of our shortcomings.

God and guru, never let me think
that you do not speak to me.
Remind me to look for you in love.

Prayer

September 20

"A prayer that is strong and deep will definitely receive God's attention."
Yogananda

Though Yogananda taught about the centrality of meditation in the spiritual life, he also stressed the importance of prayer. His teaching on prayer helped me to deepen my prayer life in ways I could not have imagined. Often we pray to God or at God, pleading for fulfillment of our desires. Yogananda teaches us to pray in God and with God. This means praying not from our surface personalities, but from our deepest, purest depths, with absolute earnestness and sincerity. Rather than being polished and polite with God, simply cry for God and guru to come to you. Such prayer immediately puts us in conscious contact with God. Praying in this manner challenges us to be entirely transparent and totally real with God and ourselves. True prayer arises from our souls and literally holds the power to move heaven and earth – because our souls are in God and God is in our souls. The ultimate prayer is not to ask God for things, but to ask God for God. When we have God, we have everything.

**God and guru, give me faith
that you always hear my prayers.**

Prayer

September 21

"Knock and the door shall be opened."
Jesus

Growing up Catholic, I was constantly encouraged to pray about anything and everything. As I began to meditate, however, my prayer life virtually ceased because I honestly thought that meditation was enough. Then about ten years ago, when I felt distressed about an issue in the life of someone I loved, I found myself spontaneously on my knees, speaking to God, Christ, and Yogananda from the depths of my heart. I was praying. Almost immediately, I experienced the palpable, intimate presence of God. Eventually, the person I was praying for did find a resolution to the problem, and I rediscovered the power and importance of prayer. Now I see meditation as the left lung of the spiritual life and prayer as the right lung. Both are essential practices for our spiritual lives. So, what is prayer? Simply put, prayer is lifting our hearts, minds, and spirits towards God. Sincere prayer creates intimacy between God and ourselves. Soulful prayer is true communion with God. If you do nothing else today, pray honestly and personally.

You have heard my every prayer.

Prayer

September 22

"We are God's children. He has to listen to us."
Yogananda

Recently, a middle aged man told me that he wished he had learned to pray earlier in his life. When I asked why, he replied, "I could have caused others and myself much less pain. I could have done things God's way instead of my way." I told him that the second half of his life would be very different from the first half! We are all God's children. We have been created to live our lives in profound intimacy with God, to share our burdens with God, and to live from God's love, wisdom, and unlimited provision. Despite this reality, when we are afraid and hurt we build self-protective walls around ourselves, hiding from God and others. In prayer, we deconstruct our walls and gradually grow open, naked, and vulnerable before the Divine Presence. What do we pray about? Everything! Prayer is letting God into the nooks and crannies of our lives, including our relationships, our sexuality, our finances, and our addictions. To be free to pray in this way, we must believe that God is unconditional love, that God will never judge us, and that God welcomes us with open arms.

I am your child.

Prayer

September 23

"Will not God give justice to his children, who cry out to Him day and night?"
Jesus

Sincere, pure prayer requires the virtue of perseverance. We must persevere -- not because God is distant or uncaring, but because we are all enveloped within layers of murky resistance. We want God's will, but we also want our own will. We want God's blessings, but only on our terms. We all want to be happier, but we don't want to change. In other words, it is easy for us to pray with mixed motives, or what Yogananda referred to as a lack of earnestness. Perseverance works in two ways. First, it cuts through our scattered will, forcing us to be very, very clear in terms of what we want from God. Perseverance in prayer purifies us and draws us into deeper and deeper levels of earnestness. Secondly, earnest prayer reaches straight into the heart of God, because God is the very essence of sincerity. Our clear and sincere prayers align us with God's clear and sincere designs for us, allowing God's loving and all-powerful will to be unleashed in our lives. Pray sincerely and perseveringly.

**Guruji, grant me the gift
of perseverance.**

Prayer

September 24

"We are God's children. He has to listen to us."
Jesus

People often wonder why they should bother to pray if God is all-knowing, all-powerful, and in charge. Human life is marked not by compulsion, but by freedom. Our lives are designed to be a partnership of loving cooperation with God. Therefore, life on planet Earth is a zone of freedom, wherein we are free to welcome or resist God's participation in our lives. Yes, God uses our mistakes, ignorance, and sins to bring about a greater good. This does not mean, however, that God chooses our choices or creates our suffering. That responsibility lies squarely on us. We are not punished for our sins, but by our sins. Sincere, selfless prayer works because it aligns us to God's loving purposes. Prayer welcomes God's interventions into our day-to-day lives. Prayer gives God permission to work miracles in our lives and in the lives of others. Prayer changes the course of history.

Thy will be done!

Living Spiritually
September 25

"Always keep your discrimination alive. Avoid those things that will not benefit you. And never pass your time in idleness."
Yogananda

As a high school senior, I had a no-nonsense priest as a spiritual director. During one of our conversations, he asked me about my prayer life. I told him that I had been busy lately and had not had much time to pray. I still remember his forceful response: "How dare you waste the precious gifts God has given you! You have a mind, a heart, and free will. Focus them on God so that you can create good things with your life. And don't come to see me again if you are not regularly praying. My time is valuable." He was right. Our minds and our hearts are great gifts, given to us so that we might bring the consciousness of God into our day-to-day lives. We must choose to be alert and steadfastly oriented towards truth, beauty, and goodness, thus allowing heaven to breathe new life into planet Earth through us. Today, stay present, don't run from discomfort, and continuously lift your mind and heart towards the guru. Don't live on the fringes of God's presence, but in the very center of the Divine Fire.

My focus is on you.

Living Spirituality

September 26

"You will know the truth and it shall set you free."
Jesus

If it is freedom that we desire, we must be unconditionally committed to the truth above all else. There is nothing wrong in wanting to be happy or in having our legitimate needs met, but if we already knew how to produce these things we would not still be seeking them, correct? Truth is the only path to abundance, joy, and all that is noble and worthwhile because truth is Divine Wisdom distilled in human form. Every day we should ask ourselves if we want what we want or if we want the truth. Yogananda tells us, "A truth cannot be created, but only perceived. Any erroneous thought of man is a result of an imperfection, large or small, in his discernment. The goal of Yoga science is to calm the mind, that without distortion it may hear the infallible counsel of the Inner Voice."

**Let my prayer be:
What is the Truth?**

Living Spiritually

September 27

"Be as wise as serpents and as clever as doves."
Jesus

If we are to become truly transformed and not merely improved, one of the first of our beliefs that has to go is the notion that people, society, and the world should be perfect. Imagine how much happier we would be if we could accept the truth that earth is not meant to be a heavenly reality! Imagine how content we could be if we did not expect perfection of ourselves or others! Imagine how free we would be if we radically accepted the fact that pain is a natural and necessary aspect of life! And imagine how free we would be if we believed that all of our challenging situations were mysteriously stamped by the will of God! We would no longer experience ourselves as victims. We would view our circumstances more impersonally, and we would be more patient with our own faults as well as the faults of others. The Divine Intelligence that runs the universe would pour through us, helping us to respond to all circumstances with wisdom, courage, and lightheartedness. We would be so free that we would hardly recognize ourselves! So stop expecting perfection from yourself and others. Stay prayerful and open, allowing the river of God's grace to take you exactly where you need to go.

**What would I be like
if I was truly free?**

Craig Bullock

Living Spirituality

September 28

"Preach the good news, but use words only when it is absolutely necessary."
Saint Francis of Assisi

Jesus asked his disciple, Mary Magdalene, "What is the most destructive, damaging, and divisive force in the world?"

After a few moments of reflection, Mary answered, "The human tongue. It distorts the truth, murders people's reputations, sows seeds of discouragement, and creates dissention among people. I am not sure why God even gave us the capacity for speech."

Jesus replied, "You have answered well. Now, tell me what is the most beautiful, most precious, and most elevating force in the world?"

After pondering the question for a period of time, Mary said, "The human tongue. It speaks liberating truths, inspires people to acts of great courage, brings hope to souls mired in despair, uplifts the downtrodden, and has the power to heal our broken spirits. The tongue is our greatest gift because it is God's mouthpiece."

Smiling, Jesus replied, "You have answered well. If anyone has ears to hear, let him hear."

Beloved, if my speech will not serve love, may I have the self-control to remain silent.

Living Spiritually
September 29

"Those who meditate deeply feel a wonderful inner quiet. This stillness should be maintained even when in the company of others. What you learn in meditation, practice in activity and conversation. Let no one dislodge you from that calm state."
Yogananda

On one of my solo trips to Assisi, I met two young Italian women and asked them to take my picture. Assuming that I did not understand Italian, one of them said that my face was ugly, and the other one laughed. When I told them, "Capisco Italiano," they were clearly embarrassed. But I was able to smile and laugh, and the awkward moment dissolved. Without a meditation practice, the ability to witness my emotional reactions, or faith in God's providence, I probably would have given them a humiliating tongue lashing. Two choices sit before us at all times: we can react habitually or we can respond from a place of freedom, compassion, and wisdom. Therefore, meditation is the most practical discipline we can ever undertake. Through meditation, we gain freedom from entrenched karmic patterns and avail ourselves of heavenly inspiration, lightness, and even humor.

**Divine Mother, may it be you
who responds to others, not my reactive ego.**

Craig Bullock

Living Spirituality

September 30

"Become so drunk with love of God, that you will know nothing but God, and give that love to all."
Yogananda

One day during my senior year in college, I woke up in a very foul mood and felt entitled to share it with everyone I met for most of the day. Later in the afternoon, I met with my spiritual director, a Franciscan nun. I talked about my lingering irritation and wanted to dig for the root of it in a childhood trauma. After listening to my ranting for a few minutes, she said, "Enough with words. This is what I want you to do: sit in front of the icon of Saint Francis in the side chapel. Breathe and gaze upon the beautiful image of Francis until your agitation disappears." I did as she requested, and after about forty-five minutes everything changed. My heart opened and God's presence became very palpable. What a lesson! If we want to heal our wounds and speak and act in an inspired manner, we have no choice but to melt into love, into the Divine Heart. The path of the mystic is the path of vulnerability and love whereby we approach God without boundaries, barriers, or protection. Only to the extent that we melt into the river of Divine Sweetness do we become fully alive and fully human.

I will sit, breathe, and gaze.

Francis of Assisi
October 1

"God is beauty, goodness, and truth."
Pope Francis

Eight hundred years ago Europe was steeped in the dark ages. Poverty, war, and despair ran rampant over God's suffering children. So God raised up a humble, joyful beggar from Assisi. Francis had neither riches nor fame to offer his troubled brothers and sisters, but only his humility and God's love. This love became an inferno of light, dispelling darkness and giving hope to those overshadowed by despair. As in Francis' time, darkness similarly envelops the world today. God has mercifully raised up another Francis: Jorge Mario Bergoglio. He humbly channels God's beauty, goodness, and love not only to Catholics, but to the whole world. His light invites us to realize that a Francis lives in each one of us because we are all created in God's image. God needs the Francis in all of us to burn robustly, boldly, and brightly. We don't have to be perfect, just humble, willing, and open. Today, simply greet everyone with warmth, understanding, and compassion. This is a great beginning.

**Francis of Assisi,
you live in me.**

Francis of Assisi

October 2

"Give thanks to God, for His loving mercy is eternal."
Psalm 107

Part of what we love about Francis of Assisi is that he was not born a saint; he experienced many of the very same struggles as you and I. In fact, prior to his conversion, virtually everything he thought and did was self-centered, and as a result he suffered greatly. The good news is that God did not abandon Francis to himself. As he was meditating before the cross in the church of San Damiano, Francis heard Jesus speak his name in a "tender voice." That gentle voice conveyed the very mercy of God: goodness, forgiveness, hope, and salvation. God's mercy elevates us and our consciousness, sets us on a new path, and resurrects our dignity. God's mercy enables us to forgive ourselves. My friends, just as God did not abandon Francis, God will never abandon you or me. God's mercy is ever with us. We just have to open our hearts and ask for help; then, we have to be little and humble enough to receive all that God wants to give us.

**Beloved, may I be small enough
to receive all of you.**

Living Grace

Francis of Assisi
October 3

"Giving love to all and seeing God's presence in everyone: that is the way to live in the world."
Yogananda

God's tender mercy saved Francis from his depression and despair. However, that was not the end of the story. God wanted more for Francis; God wanted Francis' heart to be broken wide open with love. So what did God do? He put a disfigured leper directly in his path. Most of us know the story. Overcoming his revulsion, Francis showed mercy by kissing the leper and then washing him and cleaning the pus from his sores. But there is a deeper level of mercy expressed in this story. Lepers were outcasts who had no legal standing; they were human pariahs. Francis was not only caring for the leper's body, but also for his heart. He befriended and humanized the leper; he restored the leper's dignity, just as Christ had restored Francis' dignity. If you are reading these words, God has welcomed you as His friend, His child, and His beloved. God is restoring your dignity. Allow God's mercy to open your heart even more by following Francis' example. Forgive those who have hurt you, see God's presence in everyone, and treat everyone you meet as a friend.

Francis, bless me that I may love the lepers in my life.

Craig Bullock

Francis of Assisi

October 4

"Francis of Assis was a great lover of Christ, and an exemplar of what a follower of Christ should be."
Yogananda

This day is the feast day of Francis of Assisi and also the anniversary of his death in 1226. It is said that people die as they have lived. As he lay dying, Francis asked his caregivers, "When you see that I have come to the end, put me naked on the ground, and allow me to lie there as long as it takes to walk a leisurely mile." Francis' final gesture was a loving expression of his relationship with God. He chose to enter eternity naked, with no possessions, close to the earth and utterly dependent on God. Shortly before he left his body, his followers heard him whisper the opening verses of Psalm 141: "When I call upon you, O Lord, come quickly to me... Give ear to my voice when I call upon you.. In you I seek refuge; do not leave me defenseless. Francis died as he lived – simply, from his heart, and entirely surrendered to God.

**God, thank you that we know
the story of Francis' holy death.**

Living Grace

Francis of Assisi
October 5

"When Francis prayed in the wilds and in solitary places, he would fill the woods with sighs, water the earth with tears, beat his breast with his hand, and, making the most of a more secret place, would speak aloud with his Lord."
Thomas of Celano

What are we to make of Francis' style of prayer? For Francis, God was not a heady theory, but an experience and a relationship. Through painful failures and prayerful longing, the walls around his heart came tumbling down. When Francis prayed he poured his heart out to Christ. He exposed his innermost spirit to God and stood naked before all of heaven. And God matched Francis in reply: God took Francis' heart and expanded it so that he was capable of seeing and loving God in all of creation. We need not imitate Francis' style of prayer, but we would be wise to be prayerfully honest, naked, and sincere in God's presence so that God can flood our hearts with the very same love and joy. Do not be afraid to be real, messy, and human with God. Your honesty will give God permission to divinize your humanity.

Beloved, take me just as I am.

Francis of Assisi

October 6

"May the fiery and honey-sweet power of your love, O' Lord, wean me from all things under heaven, so that I may die for love of your love, who deigned to die for love of my love."
Francis of Assisi

In Christ, Francis found his great love, his heart's treasure, and his life's purpose. Nothing would become between him and his new-found love. Therefore, he took a vow of radical poverty, not because money or material possessions are inherently evil, but because he wanted to remain completely available to God. For most of us, such a literal vow is not practical, yet the spirit of the vow applies to all spiritual devotees. The spirit of poverty means that God is our first love, and that all of our choices serve the purpose of deepening our conscious contact with God and attuning ourselves more intimately to God's love. Though these might seem like a great sacrifice, they are not because the deepest, most exquisite of loves – God's love – is motivating us. The great paradox of Francis' life is that in his giving up of everything, he received everything: the perception of God in all of creation.

Your priceless love makes me ready to release all my possessions to you.

Francis of Assisi
October 7

"The Lord has called me into the way of simplicity and humility. He told me I am to be a new kind of fool in the world."
Francis of Assisi

It is easy to romanticize Francis' life, but the truth is that he experienced many challenging trials, just as we all do. His family, friends, and church often saw him as a complete fool. Yet Francis displayed great courage in the face of these adversities. He stayed the course and became one of the greatest spiritual warriors of all time. If we are to remain faithful to God's calling and if we are to receive all that God wants to give us, we have to accept the fact that there will be resistance. If God calls you to a certain path, task, or way of life, don't let the murmurings of others pull you down. Stay humble before God, guru, and your mentors, and ignore the limitations of small-minded people. Keep the eye of your soul on God. Faithfulness to God's calling, especially in the midst of trials, is the source of our strength.

May I be unafraid to remain faithful to my calling.

# I Am a Soul

October 8

"How easy it is to pack the day with foolishness; how difficult it is to fill it with worthwhile activities."
Yogananda

There are always only two paths before us: the way of the ego or the way of the soul. The egoic path leads to tyranny; the soulful path, to freedom. We must understand the difference between these two roads! The voice of the ego is an endless stream of compulsive chatter, recycled concepts, and intrusive thoughts; it has no capacity to impart peace. On the other hand, the soul does not think thoughts. It simply reflects the light of God's wisdom and love. If we are vigilant and prayerful, the soul's wisdom will bubble up into our awareness as inspired intuition. The soul always offers the scent of peace, even in painful or challenging situations. Today, make the effort to live consciously by patiently and persistently directing your attention to truth, beauty, and goodness. At first, such alertness can be tiring, uncomfortable, and even painful. But if you persist, soulfulness becomes a way of life, and you will find your mind calm and still, increasingly illumined by God's light and wisdom.

The soulful path is calmness, stillness, light and wisdom.

I Am a Soul
October 9

"Give gifts of love and peace to those whom others pass by."
Yogananda

One of the surest signs that the ego is running wild is the impulse to criticize, judge, and condemn everyone, including ourselves. The ego searches for faults and finds gratification in people's imperfections. The ego's motivation is never to heal or to help, but rather to experience a sense of personal superiority. By contrast, the soul naturally exudes compassion, loving kindness, concern, empathy, and warmth. The soul does not deny destructive behavior or toxic attitudes, but rather understands that underneath our foolishness is an ocean of hurt, pain, and fear. The soul knows that only in the context of unconditional love can we have the courage to face our own brokenness. Remember, neither God nor the soul condemns. They only love, because they are love.

Divine Mother, my ego knows not what it does. Give me awareness and compassion.

I Am a Soul

October 10

"Whatever you do to the least of my brothers and sisters, you do unto me."
Jesus

The ego is absolutely tribal. Everywhere it looks, it sees and relishes division: blacks and whites, saved and unsaved, liberals and conservatives, insiders and outsiders. But through the lens of the soul, everything and everyone belongs. Catholics and Protestants, Jews and Gentiles, believers and unbelievers, light and dark skinned peoples: we are all invited to break bread at the table of God's presence. The soul acknowledges individual differences, but it also knows that we are not different in any essential sense. The soul's mission is neither division nor sameness, but unity. Additionally, the soul's mission requires silence. In prayerful silence, all conceptual, theological, and cultural differences dissolve. If we nurture this unitive silence and bring it into our daily lives, we will see and celebrate unity in the midst of glorious, God-given, uniqueness.

My brother and my sister, we are uniquely different but also the same.

Wounds
October 11

"Carry your wounds gracefully."
Father Richard Rohr

We all have wounds, but the good news is that we are not our wounds. Remember, we do not have a soul; we are a soul. Our souls can never be wounded or broken because they are the very image of God. For this reason, we can face and feel our woundedness, not from a place of stoic willpower or emotional drama, but from the wise and expansive silence of the soul. Such soulfulness not only makes our pain more manageable, but it also deconstructs all of the stories we tell ourselves about our pain. As we spend more and more time in loving contact with our souls, we stop naming our woundedness as "bad," and we stop naming ourselves as victims. We begin to realize that within our woundedness lies a hidden blessing, that there is a loving plan, and that our suffering is meant to propel us into the arms of God. The more we live from the consciousness of the soul, the less we suffer.

**May I carry my wounds
gracefully and respectfully.**

Wounds

October 12

"God has arranged all of this."
Yogananda

If we are to carry our wounds gracefully, we must accept a fundamental spiritual truth: our lives unfold within God's loving and intelligent design. This means that the wounds we have are the exact wounds we need in order to grow and revolve. What if there is no such thing as coincidence? What if our point of weakness or struggle is the exact vulnerability we need in order to best allow God to flood our lives with truth, beauty, and goodness? Our task, then, is not to ask.

"Why?" but rather, "God, what are you trying to teach me through my pain? What is it that I need to do, to hold, or to experience?" Without indulging or dramatizing your pain, make room for it and do not be afraid to feel it. Prayerfully, let your pain be your friend and guide. The road to heaven must necessarily pass through hell.

**Beloved, what do you
want me to learn?**

Wounds

October 13

"I glory in my powerlessness, for God's power is manifested in powerlessness."
Saint Paul

All of us feel an impulse to deny that we are wounded because we often carry deep levels of shame about our woundedness. The essence of this shame is the emotionally charged belief that we are defective or bad and that our wounds are somehow our fault. As long as shame dominates our feelings and attitudes about our wounds, it is impossible to carry them gracefully. So what is the truth about our woundedness? First, all of us are wounded; it is the human condition. Secondly, we did not create our woundedness. Whether we call it karma, original sin, or maya, we are all born into it. There is no one to blame! Finally, who says that wounds are bad? When our wounds are accepted, embraced, and surrendered to God, they become portals through which grace, wisdom, and compassion flood our lives.

**Fill the cracks in my heart
with your love.**

The Present Moment

October 14

"It is heaven all the way to heaven."
Catherine of Genoa

Give up the search for God, now! You and God already share the same body, the same heart, the same soul, the same life, and the same consciousness. Spiritual growth is not about attainment or achievement, but it is about uncovering what has been there all along. Underneath all of our activities and accomplishments is God's simple presence which sustains, inspires, empowers, and guides us. When we view ourselves as the architect of our lives, we erroneously think we are doing it all on our own. But when we truly recognize that God is the "doer," we automatically relax. Each moment of our lives becomes a point on a map, designated by God since the beginning of time, which serves our highest evolution. This realization allows us to stop resisting the moment and to embrace what is in front of us. Live each and every moment as though you chose it, because your soul has chosen it with God.

**I will never be closer to you
than I am at this moment.**

Living Grace

The Present Moment

October 15

"When Francis was granted a visitation from the Spirit, he followed it as long as the Lord allowed, and he enjoyed the sweetness offered to him. He would stand still and render this new revelation fruitful, not receiving the grace in vain."
Saint Bonaventure

God's Spirit and God's Goodness visit us many times a day. Part of the spiritual life is learning to recognize and celebrate these visitations. They come in simple, very human forms: a kiss, a smile, a word of encouragement, a joke, and a good night's sleep. These visitations can also come as inspirations, wisdom, guidance, joy, light, expansive love, or an answered prayer. Our part is simple: stay present, alert, open, and silent so that the visitations may ripen within us. The more we give them space, attention, gratitude, and love, the more often they come. Eventually, we will realize that our entire existence is one large, uninterrupted vision.

**May I always be ready
to stop and recognize you.**

The Present Moment

October 16

"Live each moment completely and the future will take care of itself."
Yogananda

We are always trying to get somewhere, achieve some goal, or experience something new, different, or better. Such striving has its place in life, but when we become obsessed about the future, we miss the moments of heaven that are right in front of us. A truly good life is nothing other than a series of loving and well-lived moments strung together. So keep it simple today. Stay entirely present, regardless if there is pain or pleasure. Be engaged with people; smile at them, and feel the joy as they smile back at you. Chew your food slowly and enjoy every morsel of it. Today, be mindful that everything you have is literally being given to you by God. Do everything you do today for God and guru, no matter how mundane. Live today as a conscious and intentional participant. Heaven is not a destination, but a way of living and loving that allows us to experience God's presence here and now.

May I live in heaven today.

Temptation
October 17

"Jesus was led by the Spirit into the wilderness to be tempted by the devil."
The Gospel of Matthew

The ultimate goal of the mystical path is not an escape into beautiful white light, but rather to become fully God-realized as a human being. As we approach a new threshold of spiritual growth, the old habits, attitudes, and moods will necessarily pull on us, sometimes with great force. This is actually a sign that we are making progress! These gravitational temptations are necessary for our growth. Resistance makes us stronger. Each time we prayerfully say no to a negative force of temptation or yes to the magnetic potency of God's grace, our spiritual will becomes more dynamic and more aligned to the Divine Will. Through temptations, God is paradoxically growing us into sainthood. Fortunately, we are never alone in our temptations. The guru is with us, and saints and angels walk alongside us and protect us. When we stumble, they will lift us up. Our job is to keep our soul's eye focused on God, no matter what.

My eyes are on you.

Craig Bullock

Temptation

October 18

"All prophets of God during their earthly incarnations were tested and had to overcome the frailties of mortal embodiments in order to attain the final state of mergence in the Cosmic Consciousness."
Yogananda

In the midst of temptations, trials, and tests, our task is not perfection but fidelity: fidelity to God, to guru, to our spiritual practices, to our moral imperatives, and to our willingness to be an instrument of God's love. Such fidelity places us in God's hands, which means that we are resting in the very center of God's loving providence. Fidelity allows God's light to penetrate to the very marrow of our bones, transforming us into light-bearers. Fidelity to the path is the path.

Set me as a seal on your heart.

Temptation
October 19

"My body shall pass but my work shall go on. Even when I am taken away I shall work with you for the deliverance of the world."
Yogananda

Of course we should try to overcome temptation and seek to triumph over our trials! We must also acknowledge that there will be times when we stumble, not because we are bad but because we are human. We must remember that God and guru are master painters, capable of using our flaws and impurities to create beautiful colors and exquisite lines. God always metabolizes our imperfections into a higher plan. At the end of the day our job is to humbly place both our successes and our failures at the feet of God and guru in a spirit of childlike trust. The victory of good over evil is absolutely certain, because God's love is the most powerful force in all of creation. Someday, we will all reap the fruits of this victory. Until then, we continually throw ourselves into the arms of a God whose essence is tender mercy.

**Beloved God, you will not waste
a single moment of my life.**

Jesus

October 20

"For God was pleased to have all His fullness dwell in Jesus, and through him to reconcile all things to Himself."
Saint Paul

At the age of sixteen, I underwent a profound spiritual awakening. From that point forward, Jesus became not merely a teacher of wisdom, but a real and dynamic force in my life. When Francis of Assisi heard Jesus speak to him from the cross, he experienced a lively power that radically changed the direction of his life and that of the entire Catholic Church. Yogananda tells us that, "Jesus Christ is very much alive and active today...he is working unseen by the masses for the regeneration of the world." And Jesus works not just for Christians, but for all of humanity. Contact with Christ or any true avatar results not in pious platitudes or mere humanitarian warmth, but the divinization of our bodies, minds, and spirits. According to Yogananda, "The Good Shepherd of souls, Jesus, opened his arms to all, rejecting none, and with universal love coaxed the world to follow him on the path of liberation."

**Jesus, may I join
all who follow you.**

Jesus

October 21

"The time is fulfilled; the kingdom of God is at hand. Repent, and believe the good news."
Jesus

Jesus called the people of his day, and us, to repentance. But what does repentance mean? Repentance is the pathway out of suffering! Pain is a part of life, whether or not we are on a spiritual path. Suffering, however, is entirely optional. We suffer whenever we are locked within our own distorted thoughts, feelings, and fears. Freedom from suffering occurs when we repent, when we allow the power of truth, beauty, and goodness to draw us out of our interior prisons and into the flow of God's liberating love. Simply, repentance is putting aside the old self and taking on the new Self, which has been hidden in God from the beginning of time. All sincere people who in mind and heart say Yes to the grace of Christ Consciousness, regardless of their religious affiliation, experience liberation. The good news is that Jesus' mission is for the entire world, not just for Christians. His God-filled presence is available to all people of good will, to the end of time.

**Jesus, you will free me
and all people from suffering.**

Jesus

October 22

"Believe the good news... The kingdom of God is within you."
Jesus

Jesus summarized his entire mission and message as being nothing other than "good news." He said this because he knew that within each one of us there is a force-field of truth, beauty, and goodness, an infinite reservoir of heavenly energy, yes, God's very dwelling place within our hearts. Jesus lovingly challenged us to live from our interior depths, so that the Divine Life could manifest in our day-to-day lives. Yogananda tells us, "One who finds within himself that 'secret place of the most high,' becomes suffused with supreme happiness and divine security." Our job, through prayer and meditation, is to continually knock on the door of God's inner kingdom. Whether we are working, playing, or serving others, a strand of our attention needs to stay consciously anchored in God's presence, and our attentiveness will allow God's wisdom, love, and strength to bubble up into our awareness as needed.

**Jesus, you know the truth
of what is within me.**

Jesus
October 23

"God is love."
Yogananda

Jesus' life embodied the truth of all truths: Love is the most powerful force in all of creation! On the cross, Jesus' body absorbed the worst aspects of our humanity in the form of irrational hate and cruel hostility. Yet in his darkest moment, the power of love surged through him as he said, "Father forgive them, for they know not what they do." On the third day he rose from the dead, palpably demonstrating that Divine Love conquers everything, even death. Love always works; the problem is that it is seldom tried. If you are reading these words, you are on a spiritual path. You should assume, therefore, that you have been given a summons. Like Jesus, you have been called to embody love in all aspects of your life. And yes, it will hurt. But it will also resurrect your noblest, most joyful possibilities. Love, however, does not come from you. It flows through you, from God who is love. For this reason, the capacity to love is born in meditative silence, because it is there that we lose ourselves in love, in God, and it is there that we become love. In the heart of every human being lies humanity's highest hope and deepest dream: that love is God and God is love.

**Love does not come from me;
it flows through me.**

Jesus

October 24

"My guru showed me how to use the chisel of wisdom to make myself into a fitting temple to receive God's presence. Each man can do the same, if he follows the precepts of divinely illumined teachers."
Yogananda

When I was sixteen, I was placed into a home for delinquent boys because I was homeless. Alone in my room at night, I would read my Bible and pray. Invariably, I would experience the comforting, empowering presence of Christ. Jesus' grace sustained me! Jumping ahead a few years, my love for Christ led me to study theology as both an undergraduate and a graduate. But sadly, my spirituality became theologically sophisticated, and Jesus ceased to be a dynamic presence in my life. Lost years! Then I discovered Yogananda and Kriya Yoga. One of the gifts that flowed from this discovery was a return to innocence and a deeper appreciation for the Guru as a source of grace, strength, and redemption. Through Yogananda, my love for Jesus and his teachings has been entirely resurrected! Paradoxically, Yogananda and Kriya Yoga are making me a better Christian. Jai Guru! Victory to the Guru! Victory to Yogananda! Victory to Jesus!

**Yoganandaji, you lead me
to Jesus with love.**

Death

October 25

"Though the ordinary man looks at death with dread and sadness, those who have gone before know it as a wondrous and liberating experience."
Yogananda

We are approaching the celebration of Halloween, originally known as All Souls Day, a day to prayerfully remember our loved ones who have passed from this life. Ironically, we live in a culture that celebrates youth and shuns meaningful discussions about death. Yet, if we want to live fully and deeply, we must make peace with our mortality, and that peace descends only in the context of God's loving providence. Death is neither the opposite of life nor apart from life, but an essential aspect of it. Everything that happens to us, including our deaths, unfolds within God's heart and God's divine purposes. Though we may not always be able to see or understand God's purposes, we can surrender to the truth that God uses everything that happens to evolve us, to expand our hearts, and to bring us into deeper levels of God- communion. Death is not an ending, but a new beginning. Our aliveness is, paradoxically, directly proportionate to our willingness to make peace with death.

The exact moment of my death will unfold in your loving plan.

Death

October 26

"It is said that that sleep is the younger brother of death. It is necessary to add: forgetting is the brother of sleep.... Forgetting reduces man to animality."
Valentin Tomberg

Most of us live in a state of relative forgetfulness. Saint Paul writes that we "see through a glass, darkly," life's possibilities, the power of truth, beauty, and goodness, and the liberating force of God's light. By contrast, the Buddha is venerated as one who lived "fully awake." He lived on the cutting edge of reality, seeing everything and denying nothing. He maintained the spirit of equanimity by embracing the inevitability of death. Once we look death squarely in the eye, recognizing that all of our heart-felt projects are going to come to a screeching halt at the moment of our deaths, life becomes very precious – never to be squandered in a sleepy, vegetative existence. Every moment holds an opportunity for engagement; every relationship, a blessing; every challenge, a wondrous opportunity. Treat this day as though it was your last. Watch how alive and Buddha-like you become. This is what it means to be a saint.

Beloved God, may I remain awake each and every moment.

Death

October 27

"Therefore keep watch, because you know not the hour."
Jesus

In the book of Genesis, the serpent essentially tells Adam and Eve that they can ignore God's wisdom without any worry, saying, "You surely will not die!" In today's parlance the serpent might say, "Don't get uptight; there is always tomorrow. Spiritual maturity, however, is recognizing that time is a wonderful gift, given to us by God. With each moment, each hour, and each day, we have the privilege of creating portraits that radiate truth, beauty, and goodness on the canvas of time. We must remember that we all have a finite number of canvases, a limited number of opportunities to do the good that God has called us to do. When we leave planet Earth, the collective force of our individual moments will be the gift we give back to the Creator and also the measure of our karmic trajectory in the afterlife and beyond. Our experience of eternity is an echo of the canvases we have created while in the body. Today is a gift; you are a gift; your life is a gift; live them with joy, wisdom, and love.

**Let me never take the time
you have given me for granted.**

Death

October 28

"Every step of the way to heaven is heaven."
St. Catherine of Siena

A wise priest once told me, "People die in the manner that they lived." For some individuals, death is ominously dark. But those who live in God face death with hopeful expectation, because they intuitively know that the great adventure continues and will only grow in wonder, beauty, and goodness. What will happen to those who die while only half-alive? God, who is unbounded love, endlessly offers His children the opportunity to nurture the divine seed within them, even after death. Those who accept God's grace after death will have to face the fears that energized their resistance to being fully conscious and loving in their earthly lifetime. Mystics refer to this process as purification. Those who refuse God's offer of illumination will continue to experience a self-created hell, because they are locked into the repetition of those attitudes and behaviors that cause them to suffer. The good news is that God's love is irrevocably, eternally extended to all souls, no matter what their present state of consciousness might be. No one is lost forever!

**Your grace and mercy
are infinite and eternal.**

Death

October 29

"Teach me to treat my death as an act of communion."
Pierre Teilhard De Chardin

Everything that God does, including our inevitable deaths, is an act of love, because God is capable only of loving. Some will protest that death is painful. To them I say that God's love is a force that will do whatever it takes to evolve us, to move us beyond our self-destructive tendencies, and to divinize us. For those who are lost and overwhelmed by darkness, death is actually a blessing. It saves them from further suffering and from deepening their karmic tendencies. God's merciful providence gives them an opportunity for a fresh start. What about those whose lives have been filled with yearning for God, who have followed God and guru to the greatest possible extent? Death for them is a step towards the fulfilment of their deepest desire, union with God. Death is God's way of emptying us of all that is contrary to Him and the means by which God penetrates into the marrow of our bones and the very blood in our veins. Death strips the potential saint of the last vestiges of the false self and resurrects the Divine Image.

**My death will bring me closer
to my deepest desire.**

Death

October 30

"In my father's house there are many rooms...I go to prepare a place for you."
Jesus

Even a devout believer faces death with a certain amount of trepidation. Yet we can be comforted by the fact that we never die alone. Brother Turiyananda, a disciple of Yogananda, said that when he was with a dying person, he would hear the angels singing, welcoming the soul to heaven. Yogananda promised that one of the Kriya Masters would be present at the time of the death of each devotee to offer a loving welcome to the astral realm. Many people who have had near death experiences speak of greetings from Christ or their guardian angel. The modern mind, caught in a web of haughty rationality, may find all of these stories merely interesting myths. But those of us attuned to God grasp intuitively the truth of life after death and the existence of heavenly realms. When the body drops, so do the physical eyes, thus liberating our spiritual sight. At that time, we will be able to clearly recognize those saints, angels, and gurus who have accompanied us throughout our lives on earth. I ask, why wait until death? In the silence of prayerful meditation, intuitively make contact with God's saints and angels now.

**In death, my spiritual sight
will be restored.**

Death

October 31

"I will spend my time in heaven doing good on earth."
Saint Therese of Liseux

A few years ago on my birthday, a client of mine suddenly said, "Your mother is here." When I told her that my mother is dead, she replied, "Obviously, but she's standing behind you. She's short, red-headed, and wearing a blue dress. She is smiling at you and wants you to know that she is very proud of you." My red-haired mother stood slightly under five feet tall, and she was buried in a blue dress. My client did not know that it was my birthday. The veil between our deceased loved ones and ourselves is much thinner than we think. When we lovingly pray for our departed ones, they experience a wave of blissful joy. When our departed loved ones, gurus, or guardian angels pray for us we may feel uplifted or inspired for no apparent reason. Every bit of our spiritual growth blesses all the people we love, even those who have left the body. Likewise, their growth enhances our spiritual transformation. Our loves, associations, and God-inspired relationships endure into eternity.

**Death never breaks
the bonds of love.**

Truth

November 1

"*Truth is exact correspondence to reality.*"
Yogananda

Each year as we approach Election Day, the level of political spin, distortion, and verbal manipulation reaches a frenzied zenith. Sometimes we wonder if anyone cares about the truth. One year in November I asked myself, "How faithful am I to the truth?" I had to admit to myself that I have a tendency to manage the truth in order to make it more palatable. The more we squeeze the truth into our own comfort zones, the more watered down it becomes, and the less power it has to bring about transformation. Truth is neither an opinion, a feeling, a group consensus, a philosophical position, nor a dogmatic doctrine. Rather, truth is the force that brought the universe into existence. It is the love of God in action, doing whatever needs to be done in order to liberate us from suffering and ignorance. Truth is the very will of God. The key question is this: do we want what we want, or do we want the truth? In the short term truth can be comfortable, but in the long run it is our security and strength.

Dear God, show me the truth.

Truth

November 2

"I am the way, the truth, and the life."
Jesus

In all honesty, none of us see reality as it actually is, myself included. We all bring to life conscious and unconscious prejudices and preferences. Often we are more interested in proving we are right rather than pursuing truth. Only a mystic of the highest order, a guru, is free to see life nakedly and purely. Therefore, if we want to be free, we must be willing to sit at the feet of a God-realized master such as Jesus, Yogananda, the Blessed Mother, or Anandamayi Ma. Their words are dripping with truth, wisdom, and light. Their presence is a powerful force field of divine energy which elevates us out of ignorance. Their love is a burning fire that purifies our minds. It is easy to connect with your guru. Begin each day by gazing into an image or icon of him or her. Prayerfully meditate on your guru's inspired words. Think of your guru lovingly throughout the day and pray for guidance. Your guru will not disappoint you.

Guruji, bring me to the truth.

Truth

November 3

"You shall know the truth, and the truth shall set you free."
Jesus

The ego has one primary drive: to avoid pain and pursue pleasure. The soul is also guided by a single purpose, and it is not happiness, but truth. When our behavior, thoughts, and emotions are driven by the pleasure principle, our lives are tossed about by the desire for ever-shifting amusements. Truth stabilizes us and empowers us to live creatively and effectively. According to Yogananda, "Truth is exact correspondence to reality." In the spirit of Yogananda we can say, "Reality is God." Our goal is not merely to understand truth with the mind, but to surrender our personal will to reality, to God. In order to surrender, we must be willing to make friends with periods of pain because the power of truth will occasionally shake our world to the core. If we have the faith to surrender completely to the truth, the truth will set us free and pave the way for more bliss than we can imagine. When things get fuzzy, breathe and pray to be guided by the truth of God's own intelligence. This is spiritual practice!

Reality is God.

Truth
November 4

"What is truth?"
Pontius Pilate to Jesus

When Pontius Pilate asked about the truth, Jesus remained silent. Jesus was not simply refusing to answer Pilate's question! Jesus gave Pilate the correct answer: silence. Truth does not come to us through logic, debate, scrutiny, or opinion polls. Truth comes in silence. Silence quiets our minds, settles our interior chatter, and dissolves our desires. Silence makes our awareness supple and tranquil. When our awareness is purified, we are better able to hear God's loving and liberating voice, not in our heads, but in our hearts and souls. Silence is the precondition for the experience of truth. For this reason, Yogananda recommended that before embarking on a new or important project, we should meditate in order to attune ourselves to God's infallible wisdom.

**Help me into silence
so that I may hear your truth.**

Truth

November 5

"Truth consciousness is the capital reality that will make the Divine Life possible. It does not fumble in its handling of things or stumble in its pace."
Sri Aurobindo

Truth is not primarily a set of dogmas or doctrines. Truth is the mind of God working in and through human history to move us to God-union. It is lovingly powerful and powerfully loving. Ignorance breeds confusion, division, and dissent, whereas truth creates clarity, strength, and unity. Truth can only manifest where there is humility, purity, and a sincere desire for wisdom. So how do we find the truth? First of all, through prayer and meditation we cultivate a level of interior silence or stillness. Then we make a choice to listen to our conscience, the small, still voice within. The spiritually mature individual does not live reactively, but guided by the voice and momentum of truth. Jesus said, "By their fruits you shall know them."

Slow me down. Stop me. Help me listen. Help me to want truth.

Transition
November 6

"When you lose your life for my sake, you gain it."
Jesus

Fall is a time of transition as nature prepares for winter. In reality, we are always in a state of transition. Nothing about us or our lives stays the same. We move from a lower state of consciousness to a higher one, always toward greater expansiveness and love. But transitions come at a price! For example, in order to experience the joys and rewards of adult life, we must surrender childish notions of happiness. At a higher level, there can be no peace without silence, no joy without discipline, no hope without despair, no faith without doubt, no love without sacrifice, no fullness without emptiness, no power without humility, no leadership without service, no freedom without obedience, and no God-realization without renunciation. At every threshold of transformation we are faced with a fundamental choice that only we can make: the willingness to die to an old way of life so that we can rise to a new, elevated existence. We are only free to make such courageous choices because we have caught a glimpse of God's absolute goodness.

**Help me to accept
that life is transition.**

Transition

November 7

"God wanted to give human beings their fullness right from the beginning, but they were incapable of receiving it because they were still little children."
Saint Iranaeus

A major life transition occurs when we approach the second half of our lives, typically around age fifty. In the first half of our lives we are driven by the need to establish ourselves in the world: we go to school, learn a trade, typically get married, have kids, buy a house, and grow our careers. While these are all good and necessary, their focus is external, and the demands of life overshadow the soul's longing for God. But as we approach the second half of our lives, we are much more aware of the cry of the soul. Often, we may face a crisis of sorts: depression, a divorce, a job loss, a health challenge, and so on. It is as if the soul is shedding its skin, getting rid of what is not necessary, and embarking on the journey home to God. Many people may seek spiritual guidance at this time. We may find that peace becomes more important than excitement, and silence more important than stimulation. Increasingly, our external lives follow the lead of the soul. God is calling us to live from the deepest layers of ourselves.

Beloved, you have always been waiting for me.

Transition
November 8

"When you resist a temptation or renounce something desired below, you set in motion forces of realization of that which correspond above."
Valentin Tomberg

As we continue to transition into the last third of our lives, there is a growing realization that we are not in charge of our spiritual evolution. We intuitively know that God is running the show, working in the depths of our souls, secretly and silently. More and more we are drawn to simplicity and stillness. We are increasingly comfortable being alone and prefer simple joys. We no longer have anything to prove, and we are willing to apologize when we are wrong. We become the presence of peace for those we love. In actuality, we live as contemplatives. Our lives are lived so as to make room for God and those we love. We take life's challenges in stride. There is less of us and more of God. What is happening in and through all of this? We are being prepared to go home.

**Less and less of me...
more and more of you.**

Transition

November 9

"There is no way that we can get away from the fact that we are God's children. We are not merely creatures made by Him. We are part of Him."
Yogananda

When we look at what is going on in the world, it is easy to see nothing but chaos. At times, it appears as if the forces of chaos are wreaking havoc on our personal lives as well. How do we reconcile the perception of chaos with the all-powerful love of God? The world's mystics tell us that creation is inseparable from God, that all of life is One. God is indeed with us, not as a sleeping giant, but as a dynamic and loving presence. Most often, however, God's activity is hidden from plain sight. Science has put forth the 'chaos theory' which states that turbulence is a necessary precondition to a higher, more complex form of existence. In other words, death must necessarily precede resurrection. Today, I challenge you to live your life as if you believed that God is acting secretly on your behalf to guide all your transitions, even if you see nothing but chaos.

Beloved God, you are in charge of all my transitions.

Grace

November 10

"Blessed are the poor in spirit, for theirs is the Kingdom of God."
Jesus

Grace exists! It is a living, breathing, dynamic reality. It is God's fresh, ever-new creative energy moving in and through us, seeking to serve our highest, noblest evolution. However, we only become aware of grace when we attain a certain level of spiritual intensity, aspiration, or passion. For most of us, such spiritual intensity develops in the context of suffering. Suffering eventually pushes us beyond ourselves and our agendas into God's life and love. In our desire to transcend suffering, we open and extend ourselves to God – which unites our will to God's will. The fruit of union with God's will is the inevitable flow of grace into our lives. Grace, which brings forth unimagined possibilities, begins the end of all karma.

**Your grace will pour
new life into me.**

Grace

November 11

"I am the vine and you are the branches...he who lives in me bears much fruit."
Jesus

Our lives are driven by either grace or force; there are no other options. Force drives our lives when we forget that God is the loving source of everything:

Earth, matter, life, food, security, power, money, relationships, sexuality, and all of the heavenly realms. Because forgetfulness breeds fear, we willfully seek to control life, and thereby create a friction of sorts. This friction produces an energetic force that is ultimately combative, antagonistic, and destructive. On the other hand, grace is the love of God moving in and through creation which gives, sustains, and expands life. Grace flows to the extent that we ground our activity in silence, attune ourselves to the guru, and respond to the guru's guidance, even in the most mundane aspects of our lives. If we are to grow spiritually and experience our full potential, we must learn to distinguish force from grace – and choose the path of grace.

**Your grace
not my force.**

Grace

November 12

"The fruit of the Spirit is love, peace, joy, endurance, kindness, goodness, faithfulness, and self-control."
Saint Paul

The footprints of grace are simple. To begin with, we let go of behavioral patterns that produce suffering. Our endurance increases – meaning that we are better able to handle unavoidable pain with dignity. There is more peace and calmness in our lives. We do not get as rattled as we used to. Our lives exude a fragrance of simplicity. We talk about ourselves less often. Life becomes increasingly clearer; we know who we are and what our purpose is. Our consciousness expands so that we are able to see the bigger picture, make room for the imperfections of others and ourselves, and experience a growing connection with all aspects of creation. We become increasingly more compassionate. Our prayers become more and more selfless, inspired, and powerful. Lastly, we walk consciously with God in humility, joy, and love.

**Your grace will fill
my soul's every desire.**

Grace

November 13

"Never count your faults. Just think whether you love God enough."
Yogananda

A civil war rages inside each one of us. There is a force which pulls us into despair, negativity, fear, jealousy, apathy, and the thirst for power. But thank God, there is also grace, which elevates us toward truth, beauty, goodness, compassion, mercy, and love. It is impossible to remain neutral in the face of these two opposing gravitational fields; at any given moment, one or the other must dominate. To avoid falling prey to force, we must practice a gentle form of vigilant wakefulness by consciously directing our will, attention, and affection toward the light of God and guru. The dynamic power of God's love is available at every moment to infuse us with heavenly energy. Bit by bit, our lives will become increasingly magnetized to God, and we will grow more and more God-like. Today, stay present, awake, and prayerful. Ask God for help when you need it. Hold the silence whenever possible; always choose the path of joy; be grateful for everything that comes; laugh often. Grace happens!

**Beloved God,
watch with me.**

Silence
November 14

"Our only satisfaction must be to live in the present moment as if there were nothing to expect beyond it."
Jean-Pierre de Caussade

It is impossible for any of us to meditate formally all the time; we all have God-given duties to fulfill. Yet, we can faithfully carry out our duties within a zone of sacred silence. We hold the silence when we do our duties in a spirit of child-like acceptance, without grumbling, editorializing, or resisting. In giving up our emotional and psychological resistance to what God has called us to do, we allow God's silence to embrace, bless, and support all our efforts. Additionally, when we perform all of our duties lovingly for God, we effortlessly detach from outcomes; the fruit of all our efforts is entirely up to God. We are off the hook! Such detachment will necessarily deepen our experience of silence, which in turn makes our work even more productive.

**Whether I am meditating or working,
my soul constantly hums,
God! Christ! Guru!**

Silence

November 15

"Be still and know that I am God."
Psalm 46

There is a difference between our silence and God's Great Silence. Our silence is our prayerful willingness to stand back and compassionately witness the strident voices of our thoughts and feelings, without becoming overshadowed by them. Eventually, God's Great Silence will descend into our silence, revealing the utter falsehood of our interior voices and bestowing upon us the peace that surpasses all understanding. Our critical voices will cease, at least for the moment, and we will experience ourselves as we really are: God's very image and likeness. The negative voices and images may well return, but with less and less power. Silence is not something we can make happen. We can only ready ourselves to receive it by our willingness to let go of our assumptions, agendas, stories, and our very selves.

**I will wait for you
to fill my silence with yours.**

Silence
November 16

"Stillness is the altar of Spirit."
Yogananda

Jesus said, "You will know the truth, and the truth will set you free." But isn't it true that much of our thinking and talking is a mixture of truth and falsehood, therefore holding very little power to bestow freedom? The activity of our minds must bow before God's silence in order to be liberated. God's Great Silence is a healing balm which frees us from our distortions. The experience of silence is universal, at one and the same time the heart and soul of Buddha's equanimity, Francis' poverty, and Yogananda's renunciation. We cannot make silence happen; we can only ready ourselves to receive it by our willingness to let go of ourselves. Then, the Great Silence descends upon us from above and calms the restless mind. A calm mind will allow God to illumine our understanding with truth. Truth is not information or facts, but rather a loving and organizing force that unites us to God and to one another. Jesus referred to this force as the Spirit of Truth. Without silence there is no truth, and without truth, there is no freedom.

Beloved, I quietly wait
for your truth to set me free.

Silence

November 17

"Never think that you have experienced the last stillness...there is no end to God's stillness."
Yogananda

Yogananda encouraged his advanced disciples to take one day a week and meditate continually for six hours. That might be daunting for many of us! Yet, we can actually devote part of a day to meditative silence without formally sitting the entire time. A day of silence can have various components: a longer period of formal meditation, spiritual reading, enjoying a silent cup of coffee or tea, a peaceful garden walk, gently stretching, spiritual painting, journal writing, and so forth. We might choose to take one day a month if one day a week is not possible. Some might consider simply refraining from talking while performing duties. Even detaching from cell phones and computers can be a start. God's Great Silence is not nothing; it is neither the absence of noise nor mere quiet. It is the space where God's stirrings begin to move through us and through all of creation.

**Beloved Guru, help me to enter your silence
by giving me the will
to make changes in my life.**

Mysticism
November 18

"I am the vine and you are the branches... Remain in me."
Jesus

Many lovers of God wonder about the difference between spirituality and mysticism. Spiritual practices give us a sense of God's presence in the form of peace, joy, love, and so forth. Mysticism, on the other hand, is the direct experience of God, beyond words, categories, or feelings. In spirituality, God is close but still at a subtle distance. In the mystical experience there is no distance: lover and beloved are one, in love. Where God ends and we begin is altogether blurred. If we undertake our spiritual practices sincerely and purely, we can bring about a sense of God's presence. By contrast, mystical union is a grace, a gift, given by God. We can't make it happen. It is given to us in God's good time. We can, however, prepare ourselves for this wonderful gift through prayer, silence, solitude, and the willingness to surrender ourselves entirely to God. In Luke's Gospel, Mary's response to the angel is a mystical prayer of the highest order: "Let it be done unto me according to thy word." We would be wise to repeat this prayer often and to live this prayer every day of our lives.

Let it be done unto me according to thy word.

Mysticism

November 19

"I was blind, but now I see."
The Gospel of John

A real mystic is clairvoyant, but this ability is not a psychic gift! The word clairvoyant means "clear seeing." Yogananda tell us, "God is the life surging within us." Mystics are, therefore, able to experientially see God's presence within others, within themselves, and within all of creation. In this context, we are all meant to be clairvoyant, to see with the eyes of God. This is where meditation and prayer become so very important. Virtually everything we do in life is motivated by necessity, the pursuit of pleasure, or the avoidance of pain. Meditation and prayer, however, are motivated by something altogether different. They are choices to be consciously awake and aware, to be radically present to reality, to be naked before God and creation. Authentic meditation and prayer bring us into contact with the really real, regardless if reality brings joy or suffering. Today, choose to pray and meditate, to be awake and aware; choose to be clairvoyantly aware of God's presence within you and around you. Bow before everyone you meet, including yourself.

**Dear Beloved God,
may I see as you see.**

Mysticism

November 20

"Whatever you ask in my name (my mission), I will do."
Jesus

While mystics might be quite active or assertive in terms of fulfilling their karmic duties, before God they necessarily stand naked and unprotected, waiting for God to take possession of them. Therefore, the mystic's life is summed up in one word: surrender. Saint Therese gives us the best definition of surrender I have ever read: "It is the complete abandonment of the baby sleeping without fear in his father's arms." Mystics have given their lives over to God entirely. Their only concern is to please God, and everything else is in God's hands. Does this make mystics impractical? On the contrary, mystics tend to be more practical than most people because they are absolutely committed to God's Reality. Therefore, when mystics move into action, they become a powerful force for transformation: they become God's voice in the world.

**My Father, may I be the baby
sleeping in your arms.**

Mysticism

November 21

"Be in the world but not of the world."
Jesus

Mystics experience great peace, great joy, and sometimes great ecstasy. But the truth is that they also undergo, at times, great suffering. Slowly but surely, true mystics release their psychological defenses. This necessarily means that their spirits become more supple, sensitive, and tender. Thus, the ugliness of the world impacts them more deeply, and they feel their own shortcomings more acutely. What to do about this? If you have ever been to a cloistered monastery, you probably noticed that it was surrounded by a stone wall. The wall symbolizes the need to keep the world's darkness on the outside of day-to-day life, so that those living on the inside can orient their spirits to God's truth, beauty, and goodness. At this point in history, there are more mystics living in the world than in monasteries. These lovers of God need to build a metaphorical wall around their exposed spirits, not by burying their heads in the sand, but by discriminating what they expose themselves to, what they allow into their souls, and what activities they choose to fill their time.

**Beloved God, teach me
how to discriminate.**

Gratitude

November 22

"Live quietly in the moment and see the beauty of all before you."
Yogananda

Gratitude is not an emotion; it is a virtue. Gratitude is the recognition of a loving, breathtaking truth: Everything we have has been given to us by God. Our very existence is a gift. We did not choose to exist! Our existence was lovingly willed by God, and our ongoing existence is lovingly, purposefully willed by God. We are perpetually held in existence by God's will and God's love. Our lives are a participation in the one stream of God's life. Creation is one gigantic, ongoing manifestation of pure, divine generosity. When we open our eyes and hearts to God's unmerited bounty, we are effortlessly plunged into mystery, gratitude, and love.

I am your gift to the world.

Craig Bullock

Gratitude

November 23

"If the only prayer you said was 'thank you,' that would be enough."
Meister Eckhart

There is only one existence – God's existence. There is only one life – God's life, and there is only one consciousness – God's consciousness. But this reality does not mean that we can call ourselves God! It does mean that everything we have and everything we are is a gift from God. Even as you read these words, God is literally maintaining, supporting, and undergirding your existence by the power of His love and wisdom. For this reason, the truly wise are forever humble, joyful, and overflowing with gratitude – because they know that God is with them and loving them each and every moment of their existence.

**Beloved, may I attain true wisdom
in knowing who I really am.**

Gratitude

November 24

"In my mother's womb you formed me...I am wonderfully made."
Jewish Psalm

God has loved each of us into existence, but not in some general, cookie-cutter sense. Rather, God loved us into existence as unique, never to be repeated reflections of the Divine Image. God has placed into your heart a precious and unique jewel which is an irreplaceable blessing to the world. Today, take the time to thank God for your existence and for the distinct gift you bring to others. Such gratitude is not prideful, but an expression of profound humility.

**Allow me to see my uniqueness
and your reflection therein.**

Gratitude

November 25

"God speaks to every individual through what happens to them moment by moment."
Jean-Pierre De Caussade

We cannot experience God's loving presence until we embrace the present moment with gratitude. Father De Caussade tells us that the answer is simple: "The events of each moment are stamped with the will of God. We find all that is necessary in the present moment." The air that we breathe, the gift of sight that allows us to read these words, the sense of aliveness that sustains all of our vital functions – all are gift. Each moment, we are plunged into the mystery of God's presence and providence. We will find God the instant that we give us the search for God, recognizing the Divine Presence which envelops us here and now. When we truly embrace God in the present moment, we recognize that we are a miracle, born of God's unbounded love. Then, every breath we breathe will naturally be filled with gratitude.

**Beloved God, allow me to find you
in the present moment
and to be grateful for all that is.**

Gratitude
November 26

"The intelligence of God is present in every particle of creation."
Yogananda

We have all had those moments of illumination wherein a vexing problem is intuitively solved, a moment of creativity inspires us to a new course of action, or a flash of intuition saves us from calamity. Most of us are smart enough to know that our limited intellects did not conjure up these moments of insight. But we often do not realize that these experiences are a participation in God's creative genius. Another way to look at it is this: we do not have intellectual rights to our own intelligence – because there is only one creative genius, God's genius. Authentic intelligence, intuition, or wisdom is always a participation in God's creative genius. So, the next time you experience a flash of brilliance, know that God is near and remember to say thanks.

God, may I be open to your intelligence and welcome it gratefully.

Gratitude

November 27

"You are made in God's image; you should behave like a god. Most people are victims of moods; unless one controls them, they will control him."
Yogananda

One morning as I went to warm up the car before driving to work, I noticed that the thermometer read five degrees below zero. I was very cold. An onslaught of negative, complaining thoughts invaded my mind, accompanied by a subtle wave of depression. Fortunately, I caught myself. I paused, took a deep breath, and thanked God that my car started, for my cozy house, for sunshine, for my warm clothes, and so on. Immediately, a sense of happiness and peace returned. I was not repressing my true feelings, but rather using my God-given freedom to focus on God's goodness and generosity. Spiritual maturity is choosing to take responsibility for one's moods and perspectives, and gratitude is one of the most effective tools for helping ourselves out of negativity.

**God, remind me of gratitude
and acceptance.**

Living Grace

God Speaks
November 28

"Speak Lord, for your servant is listening."
First Samuel, 3:10

The very first time I held my grandson Noah, I spoke to him. Every time I see him I can't help myself; I am compelled to tell him in words how much I love him. Since we are made in God's image, this must mean that God speaks to us, unceasingly! And to take this truth a step further, God does not address us generically, in some kind of mechanical or impersonal manner. Rather, God addresses our specific hopes and dreams, our exact challenges and sufferings. Jesus, Francis, and Yogananda lived their lives listening to God. Were they simply naïve? Certainly not! Here is the challenge: if we dare to believe that God speaks to us, then we are compelled to listen and to let God into the nooks and crannies of our lives. Are we able to bear that much intimacy, to let go of that much control, to live our lives as a dynamic marriage with our creator?

**When I cannot let go,
beloved, help me.**

God Speaks

November 29

"This is my whole desire, that my heart be united to Thee."
Thomas à Kempis

God does indeed wish to speak to us. This reality begs yet another question: when God does speak to us, what are we actually hearing? We are actually hearing something we might not expect: God's prayer for us. Contemplatives have referred to this dynamic as the "Hearing of Prayer." When God speaks to us, we are actually hearing heaven's highest hopes, dreams, and intentions for us. All of God's prayers for us contain our highest and ultimate good. Yet it is God's prayer and not God's demand because we are free to ignore it or reject it. When we say "yes" to God's prayer, to God's will for us, we are actually answering God's prayer. Clearly, the answering of prayer flows both ways: from God to us, and from us to God. If we are wise and want to be happy and receive heaven's best blessings, we will grant God His prayers for us. We will say, with Mary, "Let it be done to me, according to thy word."

My prayer flows to you;
your prayer flows to me.

God Speaks
November 30

"The kingdom of God is within you."
Jesus

If we are honest with ourselves and if we have any degree of interior silence, we will readily recognize God's voice percolating within us: it is called conscience. Conscience is not, however, the neurotic voice of self-reproach. Rather, conscience is a divine GPS system. When we are moving in the wrong direction, our conscience informs us through discomfort and a level of legitimate guilt. When we are in the flow of God's voice we experience peace, joy, and a sense of wellbeing. The more we listen to our consciences the more creative, personal, and intuitive they become. Sooner or later we have to stop looking for God's voice on some distant mountaintop: the voice of God and guru are within us, at all times! Yogananda tells us that when he is "...only a memory or a mental image, or a silently speaking voice...I will smile in your mind when you are right. And when you are wrong I will weep through my eyes, dimly peering at you in the dark; and I will whisper to you through your conscience."

**God and guru,
guide me.**

Craig Bullock

The Guru

December 1

"In a Christ-like guru, the love of God Himself is made manifest in human form."
Yogananda

Christians have entered into the liturgical season of Advent, wherein they prepare to commemorate the birth of Jesus. Jesus was more than a prophet, a teacher of wisdom, or a holy and pious Jew. Jesus was and is a divine incarnation of the highest order, a God-realized guru, and an embodiment of God's all-powerful love. When a figure like Jesus enters human history, he brings not only inspired wisdom, but divine power, grace, and energy. His God-saturated consciousness is a transformative force within the world, offering us the possibility of furthering the evolution of our individual lives and the life of the entire human family. Spiritual vibrations are very high during Advent and Christmas, so we must neither sentimentalize Christmas nor lose ourselves in meaningless holiday activity. In meditation, in prayer, in service, and in celebration, commune with Jesus and allow the Christ Consciousness to penetrate into nooks and crannies of your soul.

**Beloved Jesus, may you find
a home in me.**

The Guru
December 2

"He who follows a God-sent guru walks in the everlasting light of God."
Yogananda

For many people, the world has become very flat. This perception means that there is no reality beyond that of the five senses, the rational mind, or those things that can be counted, measured, and analyzed. Such a world is devoid of mystery, awe, grace, and magic. The good news, however, is that there is indeed a world beyond our physical dimension. This world, full of splendor, beauty, and light, is more real than our own. As you look ahead to Christmas, don't reduce Jesus or any of God's enlightened emissaries to simply being wise men or women. They are portals into a higher consciousness who desire to lead us into love, light, and liberation. They inspire, illumine, and enrich us. Rather than taking us out of the world, they initiate us into God's world, creating within our own lives the marriage of heaven and earth.

**May I see mystery, awe, grace, and magic.
May I always believe.**

The Guru

December 3

"Through the guru, God the silent one talks openly."
Yogananda

We humans tend to make a mess of the world and own lives. Since our limited, distorted consciousness created our problems, that very same consciousness cannot solve our problems; we need a higher, transcendental consciousness. If Jesus, Krishna, Francis, or Yogananda simply represent a level of human consciousness, then we do not have to take them too seriously. But these divine avatars are not merely human. They embody God's consciousness, full of absolute truth, beauty, and goodness. We would do well to listen to their words, to absorb their wisdom and to align our lives to their lives. Today, take a line from Jesus or Yogananda and read it slowly, prayerfully, meditatively. Then, go into silence for a moment or two. Allow the God-inspired consciousness that birthed the words to penetrate your will, your heart, and your mind. Read the words again, breathing them into your soul. Take them with you as you travel through your day. Make this prayerful reading a daily practice, and watch with wonder as God recreates your life.

**Divine Mother, I am eternally grateful
for the precious words of my gurus.**

The Guru
December 4

"You are my disciples if you keep my commandments."
Jesus

When we put ourselves in charge of our own transformation or enlightenment, we only become more self-centered. We can create order and rational thinking in our lives which will foster a level of stoic peace, but stoic peace is not God's peace. Only God can impart God consciousness to us, almost always through a God-realized person. Sooner or later we must surrender to God and guru. Therefore, these avatars and saints matter: Jesus, Krishna, Yogananda, Francis, Babaji, the Blessed Mother, and all other great saints. Likewise, all holy days, including Christmas and Hanukkah, matter. These avatars, saints, and holy celebrations matter because they embody grace, divine energy, and heavenly favor. Practically speaking, we must be willing to sit at the feet of a spiritual master and listen and learn. We must be willing to have God empty us of ourselves and love us into freedom.

**May I truly honor
each holy day.**

The Guru

December 5

"I am the vine; you are the branches. If you remain in me and I in you, you will bear much fruit."
Jesus

How do we make contact with Christ (or any other divine emissary) when he is no longer physically present? As a starting point, remember that Jesus promised to be present to planet Earth until the end of time. His consciousness is available to all of us, regardless of any or no religious orientation. Yet Jesus will never impose himself on us without our loving, consistent effort to establish conscious contact with him. Without a degree of silence we cannot know or intuit spiritual guidance, so, as always, prayerful, meditative silence is how we begin. Slowly but surely, the very consciousness of Christ will stabilize your consciousness; your mind and heart will merge with his mind and heart! Yogananda, who deeply revered and loved Jesus, teaches us: "Jesus Christ is very much alive and active today...he is working unseen by the masses for the regeneration of the world...He is deeply concerned for mankind and wishes to give his followers the means to attain divine freedom of entry into God's infinite kingdom."

**Yogananda, you love Jesus
and inspire us to love him too.**

The Guru
December 6

"It is not enough to imitate Christ. We must become Christ."
Mother Teresa

Though God is ultimately beyond anything we can conceptualize or categorize, God enters creation as a purposeful, intelligent force. Yogananda refers to this intelligent force as Christ Consciousness. Jesus and all truly illumined masters are so lovingly surrendered to God's purposes that God fully surrenders His wisdom and love to them. Therefore, they become God bearers, divine incarnations, true gurus who bring God to us and us to God. They are literal portals into divinity. What is even more wondrous is the fact that it is God who has called us into our sacred relationship with the guru. Our response is always a response to God's gracious initiative. Jesus never said "worship me." He did say "follow me." To lovingly follow Christ is to surrender ourselves so deeply to God, that God surrenders the deepest mysteries of His Christ Consciousness to us.

**Divine Mother, you have called me
into sacred relationship with my guru.**

The Guru

December 7

"The friendship that exists between guru and disciple is eternal."
Yogananda

Psychologists tell us that couples who have been married for a long time actually begin to resemble each other. This is so because the human heart is constructed in such a way that it takes on the qualities of those people, attitudes, and activities to which we give ourselves. Simply put, we become what we love. There are many good reasons to have a relationship with a God-realized guru, but none is more important than the fact that the more we love the guru, the more we become like the guru. Francis of Assisi gives us a perfect example. Over time, his attention, affection, and activities were entirely focused on Christ, so much so that he became known as a second Christ. This is not just a metaphor! Two years before he died, the wounds of Jesus appeared on his body and remained until he died. Whatever we love absorbs us, our consciousness, into that. To the extent that we love God and guru, the more we are metabolized into Divinity.

Beloved guru, may there be always less and less of me and more and more of you.

Following the Star
December 8

"By day the Lord went ahead of them in a pillar of cloud to guide them on their way and by night in a pillar of fire to give them light, so they could travel by day or night."
Exodus 13:21

The Jewish tradition of Hanukkah is a celebration of the victory of light over darkness. In both the Jewish and Christian traditions, light is a manifestation of God's presence and the means by which we overcome the powers of division, despair, and depression. The significance of light should never be reduced to metaphor or myth. Without sunlight there is no physical life on planet Earth. Likewise, without spiritual light there is no human warmth, enlightenment, or peace. Hanukkah commemorates an actual historical event: the Jerusalem Temple was reclaimed from foreign powers. When the sacred flame representing God's presence was re-lit, it burned miraculously for days on end. Ultimately, the temple is your heart and my heart. Through prayer and meditation, God's light pierces the dark corners of our hearts, chasing away our fears and disordered attachments, re-establishing the light beam of divine wisdom and love.

**I want to walk
as a child of the light.**

Craig Bullock

Following the Star

December 9

"The adoration of the wise men is far more significant than merely another scene of pageantry recognizing the holy birth. It was the defining stamp of God placed on the life of Jesus."
Yogananda

God perpetually comes to us, taking birth in our day-to-day lives and in the flow of human history. God invariably comes to us as a star in the form of heavenly light. Yet we often miss this celestial light because the eye of the soul is fixated on our own projects and preferences. In contrast, the three wise men were stargazers, and their well-developed spiritual intuitions led them to focus beyond themselves, to God. They perceived God's presence as the light of Christ Consciousness in and through their interior silence. If you and I gaze for too long into the darkness that is presently manifesting in the world, we will be overshadowed by despair. Through prayer, meditation, and compassionate service, we are called to be stargazers, light-bearers, men and women of enlightened wisdom. Do not deny the presence of darkness, but view it only out of the corner of your eyes. As the three wise men, we must gaze directly into God's marvelous radiance which is always before us, even when we think it is not.

May I always look for your light.

Following the Star

December 10

"I am the light of the world. He who follows me shall not walk in darkness, but shall have the light of life."
Jesus

If the Star of Bethlehem, God's transforming light, is to make a lasting impact on our lives and in the world, we must humbly acknowledge that our consciousness is often mired in the darkness of ignorance, fear, and misguided passion – a recipe for suffering. Therefore, it is not enough only to look with wonder at the Star of Bethlehem; we must allow the light of Christ to penetrate our heart, our imagination, and our will. How do we do this? Yoganandana gives us a clear and practical map. We must daily ennoble and beautify our interior world with cheerful thoughts, with God thoughts, with the words of enlightened saints. Secondly, we must aspire to truth, beauty, and goodness, as we seek to have our will inspired by Christ Consciousness. Finally, we must cleanse our consciousness in divine wisdom through meditation. Morality, right living, spiritual concepts, and enlightened teachers point us toward the experience of God, but only in the silence born of meditation will we have the direct experience of the Star of Bethlehem.

It is not enough merely to look at your light; I want your light to fill me.

Following the Star

December 11

"There is a very strong indication…that the wise men from the East who made their way to Jerusalem were, in fact, great sages of India."
Yogananda

Let us remember an important truth: Jesus was not the first Christian. He was a mystical Jew. Christianity is the religion that has attempted to explicitly embody his teachings, his light, and his grace. The three magi were neither Jewish nor converts to Christianity. Rather, they sought to enter into Jesus' God-illumined consciousness, which is the meaning of the word "worship." In other words, Jesus does not belong to any single group, but to the whole world. He stands before the human race as both savior and brother, revealing what is possible for all of us. His grace, radiance, and presence still bless us and still inspire our spiritual transformation. When the world's religions are at their best, operating as a force for truth, beauty, and goodness, rest assured that it is the Christ Consciousness working through them. Jesus did not come to divide us, but to unite us. May unity begin with you and me, today!

**My Jesus, you belong
to all humanity.**

Following the Star

December 12

"The light-force which emanates from the star is hope.... Hope is what moves and directs spiritual evolution in the world."
Valentin Tomberg

The shocking violence that has been exploding the world over repulses us all. There are many reasons for our repulsion, but chief among them is the spiritual truth that we all carry within us: the memory of Eden and of God's loving vision for the world. Now let us return to the three wise men. The Star of Bethlehem was no ordinary light, but a manifestation of God's light and presence, which radiated truth, beauty, and goodness. The force of this radiant light became a source of hope for the wise men: it pierced the darkness of their times and resurrected their soulful memories of paradise. Authentic hope is not just optimism or wishful thinking, but the force of divine light which resurrects our capacity to re-create God's vision for ourselves and for the world. Today, turn the gaze of your soul not on the darkness, but on the light. Pray, meditate, and choose to see the good in others and in yourself. God has called us to be light bearers!

**You have implanted your dream
for the world in my heart.**

Craig Bullock

Following the Star

December 13

"Magi from the East came to Jerusalem and asked, 'Where is the one who has been born? We have seen his star and have come to worship him."
The Gospel of Matthew

We can learn something very practical from the journey of the wise men. They shared spiritual insight with the wrong person, King Herod. The result was the slaughter of the innocents after Herod ordered the killing all the male babies living in the vicinity of Bethlehem. God's light-filled presence will also inspire us to embark on a journey. For most of us, this journey is not geographical in nature, but spiritual, interior, and deeply personal. This journey takes us away from egoic consciousness, fearful constriction, and from our belief in separateness – precisely that which motivated Herod to wreak havoc on innocent people. The enlightenment we seek, the freedom we desire, can only come to us in and through God's light, or what Gandhi and Dr. King referred to as 'soul-force.' Before you make any big decision, resist the temptation to rely only on human intelligence or institutions. Follow the star by entering into meditative silence, prayerfully reading the scriptures, and asking God and guru for guidance.

I will stop and listen.

Living Grace

Following the Star
December 14

"On entering the house, they saw the child with Mary his mother, and they knelt down to worship the child. Then they opened their coffers and presented him with gifts of gold, frankincense, and myrrh."
The Gospel of Matthew

From the very beginning of their journey, the three wise men pursued one goal: to worship Jesus. True worship in the biblical sense has nothing to do with external gestures or wordy praise. When we worship, we enter into communion with God. We experience the divine presence within ourselves and recognize our underlying oneness with the Christ Consciousness. Worship is much more than a quaint custom. It is an existential necessity because we become what we worship and what we love. Scripture tells us that part of the wise men's worship was opening their treasure chests and offering all of the contents to Christ. Likewise, if we are to truly worship God, we must place all that we treasure at the feet of God and guru, holding nothing of ourselves for ourselves. When we empty ourselves in this way, we allow God to divinize our most soulful, heartfelt hopes and to fashion us into the image of the Christ.

**All that I have and all that I am
is for you.**

Craig Bullock

The Shepherds

December 15

"And there were shepherds living out in the fields nearby, keeping watch over their flocks at night."
The Gospel of Luke

In announcing Jesus' birth, the angel of the Lord did not appear to kings, politicians, or shakers and movers, but to simple, uneducated, and poor shepherds. There is great wisdom in this fact for all of us to ponder. Hearing God's voice requires a level of humility and littleness, because God always speaks in quiet, hushed tones. Undoubtedly, the shepherds never studied theology or quantum physics, but I am willing to bet that they had childlike faith in God's providence, prayed with utter sincerity, and lovingly tended to their God-given duties. For us, too much noise hampers our ability to hear angelic voices; too much sensual stimulation overshadows our attunement to spiritual guidance; and too much artificial light blocks our capacity to perceive God's subtle but all-powerful light. The Christmas message is clear: God is not seeking to build an army of the rich and worldly, but a family of simple, childlike lovers.

**How can I be
a simple shepherd this night?**

The Shepherds
December 16

"The true secret of spiritual truth lies in the cave of stillness."
Yogananda

Until the age of sixteen, I grew up in the inner city. Because of the glare of city light, I never appreciated the brilliance of a star-filled night. When I moved to my foster family's farm where there was no competing artificial light, the luminosity of the night sky mesmerized me. It took darkness to help me to see celestial light! If we want our lives to be illumined by God's light, the Christ Consciousness, we must embrace the path of the shepherds. The shepherds kept watch at night by remaining in a state of vigilance. Keeping watch is not the anxiety driven compulsion to obsess, perseverate, or analyze everyone and everything. It is a childlike commitment to curiosity, wakefulness, and presence. Keeping watch, however, must be grounded in the night. Night effortlessly darkens the ego-stimulating glitter of opinions, half-truths, and personal agendas. The darkness of night paves the way for our capacity to perceive heaven's illuminating light, helping us to see as God sees, which brings us enlightenment, joy and freedom.

I will not avoid the darkness of night, but practice my vigilance.

Craig Bullock

The Shepherds

December 17

"An angel of the Lord appeared next to them, and the glory of the Lord shone around them, and they were afraid."
The Gospel of Luke

As the shepherds watched in the dark of night, something magical occurred: they became aware of an angelic presence. Their prayerful silence and the darkening of their personal wishes opened the door of their awareness to a heavenly realm. The shepherds' experience is not a quaint myth of a bygone era. Literally, there are higher, non-physical spheres of intelligence, energy, and power that interact with our physical dimension, providing us with inspiration and guidance. Don't we need all the help we can get on planet Earth? Before human consciousness experienced a fall from grace, heaven and earth interacted in a complimentary manner. The more balanced our lives become, the more we cultivate prayerful silence, and the more we let go of our own agendas, the more intuitively conscious we become. Heavenly inspiration actually becomes a normal part of our day-to-day lives and we are never alone.

**May I always be aware
of the angelic presence all around me.**

The Shepherds
December 18

"The angel said to them, 'Do not be afraid. I bring you good news that will cause great joy for all the people.'"
The Gospel of Luke

Because we have lost touch with God's goodness, strength, and love, we believe that it is up to us to single handedly manage life's unpredictable movements. This mindset amounts to a recipe for anxiety, not to mention a profound sense of personal inadequacy. The angels, however, tell the shepherds and us to let go of fear. They know that God's presence among us is being deepened in and through the birth of Christ. Saint Paul writes, "If God be for us, who then can be against us?" This is not to say that we will never again feel fear. What it does mean is that we do not have to be overshadowed by fear, that we can choose a path of serenity in the face of calamity. Yogananda teaches us that "When subconscious fears repeatedly invade the mind…it is an indication of some deep-seated karmic pattern. The devotee must strive even harder to divert his attention by infusion of his conscious mind with thoughts of courage. Further and most important, he should confide himself completely into God's trustworthy hands."

**Because you are for me,
who can be against me?**

Craig Bullock

The Shepherds

December 19

"How privileged we are to understand so well the divine paradox that strength rises from weakness; that humiliation goes before resurrection; that pain is not only the price but the very touchstone of spiritual rebirth. Knowing its full worth and purpose, we can no longer fear adversity. We have found prosperity where there was poverty; peace and joy have sprung out of the very midst of chaos. Great indeed, our blessings!"
Bill Wilson, founder of Alcoholics Anonymous

In the face of personal challenges and the enormous challenges confronting the world at large, it is easy to feel overwhelmed and anxious. The Christmas message, however, presents us with a more enlightened possibility: God, not you, me, or our political leaders, is in charge of everything: your life, my life, and the entire world. And though our capacity to get ourselves into trouble appears to be endless, God's ability to bring good out of our self-destructive tendencies is absolute. We just have to recognize that there is a power greater than ourselves and prayerfully surrender ourselves over to that power again and again, until our peace of mind is restored.

**Beloved God, I surrender my life
and my will to your power.**

Living Grace

The Shepherds
December 20

"Suddenly a great company of the heavenly host appeared with the angel, praising God, saying, 'Glory to God in the highest heaven, and on earth, peace.'"
The Gospel of Luke

Here is a spiritual truth that is relevant at all times and in all places: The grace and energy needed to move a mountain must be greater than the size and strength of that mountain. Given the collective consciousness of the human race, the mountain of fear and divisiveness standing between us and true peace is formidable. Our good will and political resolve is not quite able to move this mountain. Something larger is needed: a Heavenly Host. Only the energy, grace, and light of heaven can move the mountains that divide us from ourselves and one another. While being wisely and creatively engaged in the affairs of the world, the eye of our souls must be filled with heaven's glory, light, and power. Otherwise, we work in vain. Instead of looking to ourselves for answers, we should prayerfully look above, to God. Only a power greater than ourselves can restore us to sanity. Remember that Jesus told us, "What is impossible for man is possible for God."

**I look to you
to move the mountain.**

Craig Bullock

The Shepherds

December 21

"Christ must be lived to be known."
Yogananda

Yogananda teaches us, "None can know Christ by reading books on theology." To enter into the blessings of the Christ Consciousness we must follow the path of the shepherds: from simplicity to watchfulness, to night, to letting go, to clarity, to the angel, to the heavenly host, to the Christ Consciousness. The process of spiritual evolution remains the same! As our consciousness expands, we can recognize the angels that are always with us; we can hear God's perpetual proclamation of glad tidings; we can remain open to experiencing God's ever-present love. However, the story does not end there. The shepherds did not become self-absorbed in their spiritual realizations. Through words and deeds, they went about spreading God's goodness to others. The bottom line is this: God is with us, God loves us, and God arranges everything to serve our highest good. The path of the shepherds is sure and true. In 1935, Yogananda wrote, "In the cradle of meditation-tuned thoughts, woven with tender twigs of devotion, behold the newborn Christ, lulled by the cooing dove of inner peace."

Lord Jesus, my heart is waiting for your birth.

Living Grace

The Birth of Jesus
December 22

"When God sees the soul...He tugs at it with a glance, draws it and binds it to Himself with a fiery love."
Saint Catherine of Genoa

Christmas proclaims a fundamental truth: Our humanity and God's divinity are two sides of the same coin. This means that everything we need to live a full, creative, and meaningful life is already within us. Jesus said, "The kingdom of God is within you." Therefore, we can begin to let go of our happiness projects. We no longer have to fix or perfect our personalities. We can stop expecting people or circumstances to bring us peace. We simply have to sink into our own souls, to fall into God, to loosen our grip on ourselves. To do this, of course, we will have to shed layers of erroneous beliefs, agree to walk through thresholds of fear, and prefer prayerful silence to the ego's chatter. We can only face these difficult tasks because God's love is stronger than our fearful resistance, inevitably drawing us into our center of our own souls, into union. Do you know that your desires are actually God's desire for you? And God's desire always wins.

Beloved God, you have given me everything I need to live a full, creative, and meaningful life.

Craig Bullock

The Birth of Jesus

December 23

"I have come that you might have life and life abundantly."
Jesus

Christmas is not about Jesus; it is about us. I am neither denying Jesus' divinity nor playing into rampant cultural narcissism. My point is this: making a fuss about Jesus is not going to make one iota of a difference in our lives if we do not take seriously our own potential to live a divine life. Jesus did not come to be worshipped. Rather, he came to reveal our true identity in God and to usher us into God-realization. The very best way to honor Jesus during the Christmas season is to embrace our God-given capacity for freedom, love, truth, and goodness. Take the time for prayer, silence, and gratitude, and do what you can to alleviate the suffering of others. Keep the eye of your soul concentrated on God and your heart surrendered to the path of love. Allow God to take you beyond your present condition, beyond yourself. Saint Catherine of Genoa writes, "When I see what God is, and the many ways He seeks to exalt us, I am transported beyond myself with astonishment."

Lord Jesus, you came to show me who I really am.

The Birth of Jesus
December 24

"If you want, the Virgin will come walking down the road, pregnant with the holy, and say, 'I need shelter for the night. Please take me inside your heart; my time is so close.'"
Saint John of the Cross

The Divine Mother is pregnant with child, and the time is so very close. She is looking for shelter, a home, a fit place to birth the Christ Consciousness. She is asking for your help. You are being called to be God's midwife. Has anyone ever told you that your soul is a womb, capable of giving birth to all of God's truth, beauty, and goodness? It is very true. You do not have to be perfect, brilliant, or even holy. You only have to be silent, open, present, still, willing, welcoming, humble, prayerful, childlike, generous, and vulnerable. Nothing else is needed. We have been told time and time again that we need God, and we do. But has anyone ever told you that God needs you? Much of the world is suffering; these sufferings are the Mother's labor pains. She is grasping your hand for help. God is hoping to be born once more in you.

Divine Mother, when you reach for my hand, I want to be near you.

Craig Bullock

The Birth of Jesus

December 25

"In the cradle of meditation-turned thoughts, woven with tender twigs of devotion, behold the newborn Christ, lulled by the cooing dove of inner peace."
Yogananda

What happened over two thousand years ago, on that first Christmas? Human evolution entered a new and profound stage. In and through Jesus, God became one of us. Yes, God is irrevocably married to the human race, including you and me – for better and for worse. This is more than an inspiring sentiment. God became human so that humanity could become divine, so that you and I could fully participate in the divine life. The good news is that our participation in the divine life does not depend on our perfection, but on God's ever-present grace and our childlike openness to that grace. Allow God to fill your emptiness with His fullness. The heavens have opened, the angels are proclaiming glad tidings to all, and celestial light is flooding planet Earth. Divine mercy has dissolved all manner of karma. Jesus has been born, and God has permanently pitched His tent among us.

**Baby Jesus,
Guruji Jesus.**

The Birth of Jesus
December 26

"God is Light."
Yogananda

Jesus is not simply a teacher of wisdom. He is the very embodiment of God's Light, which is literally a dynamic force that dispels our ignorance, purifies our hearts, and reorganizes our lives. Jesus does not give us clever words. Rather, he seeks to initiate us into the stream of Divine Light in order that we may enjoy a robust life overflowing with truth, beauty, and goodness. During the Christmas season, this light is particularly strong. While meditating today, gaze on an icon or image of Christ. Prayerfully repeat Yogananda's mantra, "God, Christ, Guru." Feel the Aum vibrating within you. Notice your mind becoming still. Sense God's aliveness pulsating through you, and enjoy the peace that surpasses all understanding. Then bring this light into all of your activities and do everything with loving attention. If you find yourself losing your composure, come back your third eye, focus on your favorite image of Christ, and consciously speak his name. This practice allows Christ to pull you into the stream of his light. It's that simple!

God, Christ, Guru.

Craig Bullock

The Birth of Jesus

December 27

"Jesus came in a darkened age...but his message of the love of God...was for all ages to come – that God is with man in his darkest moments as well as in enlightened times."
Yogananda

The birth of Jesus proclaims a truth that is relevant every day of our lives: God is fully embedded in the human condition. This means that God is present to us not only in glorious moments, but in the dark and painful ones as well. If God is present to us in our dark and painful moments, then we are never beyond the grace of heaven's helping hand. When Yogananda's disciples would come to him for advice, he seldom gave it in any traditional sense. Rather, he would tell them to place their attention on the third eye and encourage them to pray and meditate. All the strength, wisdom, and love we need to navigate life's challenges are always available to us, because God is not only with us; God is within us. Remember the words of Jesus: "Seek first the kingdom of God and His righteousness, and everything else you need will be added unto you."

Jesus, you are always available to me.

Transformation
December 28

"One should not take his troubles too seriously, lest they darken his unconscious mind."
Yogananda

As a new year approaches, we are all inclined to make resolutions. I am going to give you some counter-intuitive advice: make a resolution to have no resolutions! I am not suggesting that you should close the door to growth or evolution. Resolutions, however, typically don't work because they are engineered by the ego. The ego has neither the strength nor the wisdom to bring about real change. All that the ego wants to do is to avoid pain and pursue pleasure – which is actually a recipe for more suffering. The good news is this: God has designed the process of life so that it naturally leads to expansion, freedom, and happiness. We just have to get out of the way and allow grace to work. In order to get out of the way, we must cultivate prayerful silence, which allows us to be present to life as it actually is. When we prayerfully let go of what we want life to be and cultivate acceptance, we open ourselves to God's wisdom and grace – the only source of true transformation.

**How much peace I could have
if I let go of the way
I think things should be.**

Transformation

December 29

"You shall know the truth and the truth will set you free."
Jesus

Most of us do not really want to experience transformation. What we want is to alleviate our suffering. The impulse to alleviate suffering is understandably human, but it has no capacity to bring about real freedom because it is steeped in fear and ignorance. The fact of the matter is that we tend to distrust reality, truth, and God. Therefore, we are always trying to direct life according to our assumptions rather than allowing it to do what it naturally does: life leads us to greater and greater levels of abundance, expansiveness, and joy. So do not run from discomfort and do not chase after happiness. Instead, seek the truth, trust the truth, and love the truth. Truth is God's voice liberating us from ignorance and leading us to freedom. Truth is grounding, strengthening, and empowering. I offer you one of my personal favorite prayers: God, show me the truth. Once we decide to humbly embrace the truth, nothing can worry us.

**Beloved Divine Mother,
show me the truth.**

Transformation

December 30

"Be still and know that I am God."
Jewish Scriptures

The transformation we seek does not come about by our attempts to transform ourselves – which are really the ego's attempts to engineer change according its own distorted perceptions. Transformation begins with stillness, acceptance, and emptiness: a letting go of how we think things ought to be. If we can prayerfully stay in this silent, interior poverty, our soul's true aspirations begin to emerge. They are distinguishable from the ego's desires in that they are inspired by the power of love and oriented towards the realization of truth, beauty, and goodness. These soulful aspirations contain the blueprint for real transformation and reflect the ultimate purposes for our lives. They are our soul's prayers and longings, directed towards God. As such, they elevate us; they inspire our imagination; they strengthen our will; they bring out the best in us; they give us joy, peace, and clarity. It takes resolve to embrace interior poverty and courage to listen to our deepest, most soulful aspirations. The fruit of this process is well worth the effort: a conscious and ever-deepening participation in the Divine Life.

**God and guru, help me to realize
the hopes and dreams of my soul.**

Craig Bullock

Transformation

December 31

"Spiritual success comes by understanding life and by looking on all things cheerfully and courageously, realizing that events proceed according to a beautiful divine plan."
Yogananda

Your life, my life, and everyone's life unfolds within God's life. God's life is moving every one of us towards a purposeful and redemptive conclusion. While our cooperation is part of the process, transformation is ultimately a matter of allowing God to be God, letting go of our imagined control, and getting out of the way. An essential aspect of this process is meditation. We don't meditate to accumulate new experiences or to develop psychic gifts. We meditate so that God can empty us of our illusions, assumptions, and fears. Meditation is an invitation to release the burden of our lives to God and to surrender ourselves into God's loving hands. Our desire for peace, clarity, and God-communion increases with each meditation, and the aftereffect gradually spreads over the entire course of our lives. Life as a living meditation and a conscious participation in divine truth, beauty, and goodness is possible for all of God's children.

Guruji, may my entire life become a living meditation.

THE AUTHOR

Craig Bullock (Isha Das) is the founder and spiritual director of The Assisi Institute. An ordained Kriya Yoga teacher with the Center for Spiritual Awareness, Craig is an accomplished writer, teacher, lecturer and psychotherapist. His diverse education includes extensive study in psychology, spirituality, mysticism and world religions and yoga.

BOOKS BY CRAIG BULLOCK

Extravagant Love: Reflections of a Catholic Yogi

The Path to Healing: Experiencing God as Love

Living in the Heart of the Divine:
Prayers of Passion, Surrender & Love

THE ASSISI INSTITUTE

The Assisi Institute is dedicated to supporting individuals who seek a deeper relationship with God. Through the harmonious integration of Kriya Yoga and mystical Christianity, we are nurturing a sacred community of meditation, contemplative inquiry and compassionate living.

For more information, please visit:
www.assisi-institute.org

4/4/17 Guru says—
"Environment is more important than will power."

4/23 "I am not my personality, my mind, my body, my past nor my problems."

4/24 C.S. Lewis —
"God is wild, you know"

5/26 Courage
Sp. life is neither an escape into Nirvana, nor a type of retirement home for mystics... But a full-fledged adventure with dangers, challenges & rewards